Global Goals for S[ ] Transformation

Volume I: Driving Awareness for a Smarter Future Towards the SDG'S

I0053996

Seema Goyal

walnutpublication
.com

INDIA • UK • USA

Copyright © Seema Goyal, 2025

All rights reserved. No part of this publication may be reproduced, distributed, or transmitted in any form or by any means, including photocopying, recording, or other electronic or mechanical methods, without the prior written permission of the publisher, except in the case of brief quotations embodied in critical reviews and certain other non-commercial uses permitted by copyright law.

Paperback ISBN-979-8-89171-212-6
eBook ISBN- 979-8-89171-213-3

This book has been published following reasonable efforts to ensure the material is free from errors, with the author's full consent.
The publisher does not endorse or guarantee the accuracy, reliability, or completeness of the Content and expressly disclaims any liability for errors or omissions. No warranties of any kind are made, whether express or implied, including but not limited to warranties of merchantability or fitness for a particular purpose, or that the Content constitutes educational or medical advice.

First Published in May, 2025

Published by Walnut Publication

(an imprint of Vyusta Platforms Private Limited)

www.walnutpublication.com

India

Unit# 909, 9th Floor, Wave Silver Tower, Sector-18, Noida - 201301

UK

71-75 Shelton Street, Covent Garden, London, WC2H 9JQ, UK

Distributed by

ZopioTail

This Book is Dedicated to All of You

Acknowledgment

This book is the product of countless conversations, collaborations, and collective insights — and it would not have been possible without the support of many individuals and institutions.

First and foremost, I express my deepest gratitude to all the educators, researchers, and policy leaders whose dedication to Sustainable development and social equity continues to inspire this work. Your vision, scholarship, and perseverance laid the foundation for this inquiry.

Thank you for your guidance, your patience, and your unwavering belief in this project. Your insights challenged me to think more deeply and write more clearly.

To the communities, organizations, and field practitioners who generously shared their experiences and time — your stories gave this book its purpose and direction.

To my family and friends, thank you for your encouragement, emotional strength, and the many quiet sacrifices that allowed this work to take shape.

Our many thanks to every reader and changemaker committed to turning Global goals into local action. It is our hope that this work serves not just as a reference, but as a catalyst for continued dialogue, innovation, and transformation.

Finally, I acknowledge the many unsung contributors across sectors — educators in classrooms, students in discussion, policy advocates in negotiation rooms — who work daily to bring the Sustainable Development Goals from vision to reality.

About the Author
Seema Goyal

Educationist | SDG Advocate | Interdisciplinary Researcher | Sustainability Consultant | Founder of SDG Readiness Platform

Seema Goyal, an Interdisciplinary researcher on SDGs in terms of Education, business and policy making, eager to reimagine the future as a more socially and environmentally just world, committed towards achieving the SDGs. With 20+ years-experience in curriculum design and assess Education sector policies, strategies and programs with a view of ensuring comparability to International best practices, smart solutions and technological advances, and responsiveness to development needs of the country.

We see the purpose of SDG Readiness Platform, as being a catalyst for change that will have an impact. It is a Platform working on SDG's and Climate crisis and aims to leave behind a legacy to inspire people and various stakeholders in this arena about solutions.

Our mission is to get the leaders to meet and learn from each other and be inspired by each other. We want to get this awareness out to millions. This is more than a book, a series of pro-planet book written for everyone -wherever you might be in the world. It is for those who want to easily understand how Climate Change is affecting the planet and who want to make small, simple changes in their everyday lives to become climate aware.

By sharing knowledge, leading by example, and creating spaces for conversation, I've found that I can engage others in meaningful discussions about sustainability. It's a journey that doesn't just involve personal commitment but also empowering others to understand how their actions, whether big or small, can contribute to a more Sustainable world.

Gandhi told us to 'be the change we want to see in the world.' This book captures that spirit, reminding us that everyone can do something to help the planet."

Contents

Chapter 1

We stand at a precipice, where the intertwined crises of ecological degradation and the erosion of democratic institutions demand not just reform, but a radical reimagining of Education as a powerful force in shaping planetary futures. Choices we face now may well determine whether Education reinforces the system dynamics that have led us to this precipice or serves as a catalyst for social-ecological restoration, renewal, and resilience. In this moment of great precarity for people and the planet, scientific and technological solutions alone are insufficient; Education must drive cultural shifts and systemic transformations necessary for ecologically just and regenerative planetary futures.

Key Insights on Education for Planetary Futures and Societal Transformation reclaims the potential of Education as a transformative force — not to reinforce the status quo, but to challenge assumptions, rethink systems, and co-create new pathways toward a thriving Earth. It calls for a fundamental redesign of Education as a space for reconnecting with the living world, fostering deep engagement and mobilizing action toward ecological and social renewal.

We invite you to be part of a Global participatory effort that bridges disciplines, networks, geographies, and knowledge traditions, situated as firmly in the humanities, arts, and Educational sciences as in place-based indigenous knowledges, applied social sciences, and foundational fields of Science, Technology, Engineering, and Mathematics. By weaving together insights from diverse knowledge traditions, this initiative aims not to only align visions and actions, but to activate new synergies necessary for fundamentally rethinking the role of Education in shaping planetary futures. No single perspective holds the answer—but together, we can spark the systemic shifts our world demands.

Never in the history of humankind have we been faced with such a stark choice: to act now or risk losing it all forever.

Just as there is no more room for new fossil fuel developments, there is no room for complacency. Every single person, business, institution and government has a role to play in preserving our beautiful planet for future generations.

What Are the 17 SDGs? A Deep Dive into the Goals for a Sustainable World

Sustainable Development Goals combine the concept of planetary boundaries with a complementary concept of social foundations. If Sustainable development were adopted worldwide, it would mean that current and future generations of people would have the resources they need. They would have food, clean water, health care, and a source of energy, all without putting stress on planet Earth's systems. There's a Global plan for this. There are 17 Sustainable Development Goals formulated by the United Nations keeping the 2030 targets in mind.

SDGs are the Global strategy for Sustainable development. They can be considered wicked problems. This means that there are no quick wins, no easy solutions available, and that we can only strive for the most optimal approach towards a solution in partnership with other stakeholders. Only if we work together, we have a chance of ending hunger, poverty, or inequality. This model developed by Carl Folke and his team from the Stockholm Resilience Center, clusters the SDGs in four layers, the biosphere, society, economy, and partnerships. Without a stable biosphere is hard to build a functioning society, and without a stable society, how can you build an economy that works for all?

The importance of the Sustainable Development Goals (SDGs) lies in their role as a "blueprint for peace and prosperity for people and the planet, now and into the future." The SDGs aim to address the world's most pressing challenges, such as poverty, inequality, and Climate Change, based on the principle of "leaving no one behind."

Achieving the SDGs requires collaboration across all sectors — government, private sector, civil society, and the general public.

- Governments play a crucial role in setting policies and allocating resources.

- The private sector can contribute through responsible business practices and innovation.

- Civil society helps monitor progress and advocate for key issues such as gender equality and climate action.

- Individuals can participate by making lifestyle changes that align with the SDGs in their daily lives.

Partnerships are crucial in making everything happen. When you design a business/Country model, you have to take these elements into account as well. The future is not so much about money anymore, it is about value creation, financial value of course, but also social value and ecological value. How to organize your business in such a way that it delivers multiple values will be a key question, difficult to answer, but also an exciting challenge for adventurer's minds. As the current world is mostly cast in money terms, for companies we talk about profit, and for governments we talk about GDP. The SDG agenda means that we need to transition from business as usual to Sustainable business models that use Sustainable finance. Is your business/Country model future-proof in this new world of Sustainable development?

To reimagine a common, prosperous future on a healthy planet, the various Volumes of this Research Guidebook calls for an inclusive approach that reflects the richness and diversity of voices and perspectives of various stakeholder groups: Researchers, Academia, Business groups, governments, cities, civil society, women, indigenous peoples and local communities, faith-based groups, academia, youth, industry, finance, and philanthropic foundations.

All major stakeholder groups are encouraged to contribute to the preparation of the 2030 Targets, including through a range of National consultations.

The objective of the Five Series is to stimulate an inclusive whole-of-society and whole-of-government dialogue on the main themes of SDGs as they relate to each National context that:

- Builds a shared Global vision on how to achieve a healthy planet and prosperity for all while accelerating progress on the Sustainable Development Goals and Multilateral Environment Agreements through an inclusive green recovery;

- Offer clear recommendations for governments, civil society and private sector on priority actions that can advance National and Sectoral policies that address Climate Change and leverage nature-based solutions;

- Amplify the voices of the poor, youth, women, indigenous groups, local communities, and other marginalized groups; and

- Influence National Regional and Global debates that consider the views of all stakeholders.

Environmental degradation and Climate Change may be the largest failures of free private markets that the world has ever observed. Governments and businesses have adopted myriad policies to solve these problems, sometimes with success but frequently with unintended consequences. Business and government will have to work together to solve the most pressing environmental challenges of our time, from Climate Change to species extinction. The Business, Education, Climate and Environment Lab supports cutting edge research, provides thought leadership, and brings together stakeholders from academia, government, communities, and the private sector to design smart public and private sector policies related to topics such as Climate Change, renewable energy, air and water pollution, waste disposal, biodiversity, and deforestation.

The objective of the Five Series meant for (Academia, Business Groups, Government and Researchers) is to stimulate an inclusive, bottom-up debate on the 17 themes relevant to each National context. The idea is to facilitate a consultation process provide a platform which is based on people's experiences and ideas for "A Healthy Planet for the Prosperity of All".

To this end, the guiding-questions provided below should allow for discussions on a wide range of topics relevant to National and Sectoral policies adapted in each context.

To stimulate a meaningful debate at different levels and with a range of stakeholders, the guiding questions may need to be adapted to the local context and different target audiences. It may be necessary to align the questions with a concept of development that is particularly relevant in the country, and with the human rights, environmental and labour rights treaty obligations to which the government has committed itself.

While adapting to local needs is an important approach, it is also important that the questions remain consistent so that results within and across country can be compared and aggregated and present in a credible and powerful way in the intergovernmental process.

A Vedic phrase asks us to "treat the world as family." In our age of Global crises—pandemics, climate crisis, crippling inequality—this sentiment is more necessary than ever. Solutions to these seemingly insurmountable problems demand new approaches to thinking and acting locally, Nationally, and transnationally, sometimes sequentially but often simultaneously.

Sustainability is our core principle and moral compass that defines and drives us as an organization: our vision is to design a world where economic, social and environmental systems are in balance.

These Series will help and guide Companies, Institutions, Government to integrate ESG performance and Sustainability strategies into their core business model, and measure the triple bottom line results generated for People, Planet and Profit.

To help companies implement the Systems and Governance to Identify, Monitor and Report relevant ESG metrics, in order to build a solid foundation on which corporate leaders can make sound strategic decisions. We progress alongside companies as their outsourced ESG support as they evolve on their Sustainability journey.

What We Do

Efforts are centred around four main axes: making information accessible, changing the narrative, promoting the Sustainable Development Goals and promoting the work of SDG Readiness Platform.

(Using digital technology by creating a website to assist the spread of knowledge and ideas about the 17 SDGs - Go to SDG Readiness Platform - www.sdgreadiness.com)

The SDG Readiness Platform contributes to the implementation of the Sustainable Development Goals (SDGs) by supporting clients in further leveraging expertise and knowledge into policy, practice and action.

Companies can then use this series and the above website framework to unlock the full potential of Education in mitigating ESG-related risks, identifying opportunities, and improving business performance.

When it comes to Climate Change, young people around the globe have employed both leadership and passion to propose and demand solutions from the adults in charge. Yet with the support of educators like us, we can empower these young people to be even more engaged and effective in this work. What can we do to better equip our students with the knowledge to deeply understand Climate Change, so they can help to develop climate solutions? How can we embed Climate Change across subjects and disciplines, to foster deep knowledge of the topic among young people? How can we help our youth become better communicators — and better advocates for climate action?

How Digital Communications can assist in spreading knowledge and awareness of the SDGs through not only content creation but also holding virtual Global Events and building connections between Experts, Institutions Globally.

Coronavirus seemed to have spread Globally incredibly fast; but I think knowledge transfer and ideas can spread even faster. And the way I would like to pinpoint this is to become part of institutions like UN SDSN, UN Academic Impact Network, University Global Coalition, Global Education coalition etc. which are the various arms for academic collaborations on fulfilling the Global Goals of the United Nations. And this could happen only Post Covid with Digital Technology.

What we also find that due to the pandemic we could actually connect much better Internationally with key stakeholders, policymakers, top architects, not only on student level but at various levels on a much bigger scale with a quicker filtration not only into our academic systems, but into other stakeholders as well.

Through the digital media we can actually connect to so many more people that we would not reach out normally to and it spreads knowledge much faster than any virus can ever [do].

Our goal is to equip and provide an in-depth understanding and skills to students and all stakeholders with a conceptual framework on SDGs for understanding the evolving field.

How to teach through the lens of the Sustainable Development Goals: Bridging the Dividé: Skills for Digital Fináncial Equity and Inclusion on sdgreadiness.com

This Series along with the Platform offers insight on how the Global Goals can provide a useful framework to guide students' learning across multiple disciplines. A seemingly irreconcilable paradigms from an integrated landscape approach perspective.

We think of landscapes as systems whereby everything is connected in some way. The SDGs provide a fantastic framework to think about such an approach. No single SDG can be dealt with in isolation as they are all equally connected in some way; thus, only by addressing them all can true Sustainable development be achieved.

The SDGs underpin the course curriculum and are dealt with in a variety of ways – from mapping the connections between the SDGs and thinking about implementation and progress on targets.

When moving to online Learning/Teaching this Platform and the series has kept a strong course framework in place covering all 17 goals keeping all stakeholders in mind like Educators, Researchers, Universities, Academia, Business groups and Governments.

Having an online repository of such resources has also proven useful, structured around the background materials, referring back to the SDG framework.

Rooting the Resources on the SDGs gives students exposure to real-world issues and problems that they can, and do, explore further. Evidence demonstrates strong correlations between Education and diverse outcomes ranging from health, climate, economic growth and wages to equity, diversity and inclusion. This Platform and the series on Business Groups explores how corporate actions, small and large, can make a quantifiable and direct impact across all aspects of environmental, social and governance (ESG) priorities.

The discussions on the Platform and Series for Academia will provide a framework for investment in Education to mitigate risk, improve corporate performance, and enhance corporate perception. while making a more tangible impact on society.

Digital technology will play a pivotal role in addressing the pressing challenges associated with Climate Change. Digital transformation is already underway and is having a significant impact on agriculture, building management, and energy, among others. We're moving towards a future where digital resource optimisation is essential for achieving net zero goals.

- Hear how we can rethink Innovation, from Design to Deployment, to make Digital Greener

- Investigate how to assess whether Digital Technologies are really green through impact assessment

- Explore ways in which the Green Digital Transformation will benefit Environment, Society and Economy

- Understand what the role of Policy, Regulatory Frameworks and consumers have in the Green Digital Transformation

With the Digital Transformation already in progress, we are seeing an increase in Opportunities that extend across all sectors.

Limitations and Challenges in using Digital Technologies for Climate

1. Scaling Innovation in Climate finance and Sustainability using Green Technologies using Web -3

2. Shortage of Skilled Manpower and the frequent regulatory changes demand a financial model for tackling Climate Change using Digital Technologies

Planning is the Starting point for Climate-Resilient Education Systems

Education is increasingly vulnerable to Climate Change, but has an important role to play in helping learning communities and Education systems mitigate and adapt to it.

Educational planning that is sensitive to Climate Change, is the starting point for climate-resilient Education systems and an opportunity for a different future.

In this sense, Education is not just a victim of Climate Change. It is part of the solution and can accelerate climate action. But Education actors must fully understand risks and know where and when to integrate various adaptation and mitigation measures into the Educational planning cycle.

Making all stages of the Planning Cycle Climate-Resilient

No matter where a country is in the planning cycle, relevant and effective measures can be put in place. This is especially true when planning represents the voices of many – e.g., National and sub-National authorities, school communities, and youth, including the most vulnerable, such as girls or young women.

Mitigation and adaptation measures should ideally be mainstreamed from the start of the planning cycle, either as an integral part of an Education Sector Analysis (ESA) or as an Education sector risk assessment. crisis-sensitive planning aims to mainstream Climate Change to ensure that all Education actors – including communities, students, teachers, and middle-tier leaders– can anticipate, prepare for, and adapt to the effects of Climate Change. At the central level, this includes creating a conducive policy framework, as well as fostering Education for Sustainable Development (ESD) through the inclusion of Climate Change in curricula and teacher training. At the middle-tier and school levels, this includes school-level contingency plans with a focus on localized climate-change threats, and the construction of climate-resilient school infrastructure.

But a Plan is Only as Good as its Implementation

To ensure effective implementation of climate-related measures, ministries of Education and their partners need to involve subnational authorities, local communities, and youth, including those most impacted by Climate Change. These should then be underpinned by monitoring plans and accompanied by evidence-based costing and financing models.

Together, Education stakeholders should conduct regular monitoring to track progress on Climate Change measures and reorient strategies considering new developments and information.

To this end, strengthening Education Management Information Systems (EMIS) to collect and analyze Climate Change data requires consultation with stakeholders from multiple sectors, including from ministries of environment and National disaster management authorities.

Around the world, college and university students have become increasingly concerned and vocal about climate action. This is a powerful and growing movement that has the potential to change the course of history, yet it is unclear that climate demonstrations or divestment protests will have the desired outcome of comprehensive systemic change to avoid climate disaster.

What is recommended is that students/activists, Policy makers, all stakeholders including academia civil society, NGOs - should together share ideas, learn, connect, and act on the Global imperative of addressing Climate Change. Offered in the context of the Global climate negotiations, ESD program can challenge student teams around the world to propose ideas for local-scale projects that will yield measurable results over a stipulated time. Accepted teams become a cohort that learns together, networks, shares ideas, and contribute to a growing body of inspirational projects that demonstrate the capacity of today's youth to lead and have an impact.

All proposals must be actionable by students without extensive contingencies and should be designed to yield measurable results over the course of six months. Proposals may reflect ongoing projects and activities so long as they are the intellectual capital of the students applying and there is a projected measurable outcome during the duration of the Forum implementation period. Students will be required to attend online workshops and encouraged to interact with each other over the Forum.

United Nations Framework Convention on Climate Change, in addition to showcasing the activities and remarkable contributions of the students of the Global University Climate

Forum, it showcases how we can and should rely on universities to teach and research while elevating the thought leadership of today's college and university students.

What does the Education sector need to do in order to respond to the challenges of Climate Change? Educators and leaders are already driving impact in their schools and communities — embracing evidence-based solutions, innovative practices, and an emerging consensus around Education as a key lever for climate action. How can we broaden that vision and scale that impact?

Conduct research on the psychological, cultural, and political factors that influence environmental attitudes and behavior teaches students; informs and engages the public through environmental journalism; and supports a Global network of organizations seeking to build public and political will for environmental solutions.

Show how schools, leaders, and communities are making an impact in mitigating Climate Change, creating collaborative learning opportunities, and advancing equity in community approaches.

"Climate Change is not a future problem; Climate Change is already happening, and it affects us all". But the most serious consequences of climate disruption are not being felt equally. Climate Change is exacerbating Educational inequality. It is now another important cause of the inequities that so many of us are working hard to address. So, we need to take action…. And with about 70 million students enrolled in school from Pre-K through postsecondary Education, making Education a critical lever for change. What we as educators, policy makers do matters.

The time is now for us to do this…. The impacts are here today. Students, families, and communities are feeling them all across the country and the world, and that is only going to increase.

Mobilize youth to accelerate recovery and rebuilding efforts from COVID-19 and gather around actions, initiatives and leadership efforts that should be recognized, celebrated and scaled up towards achieving the SDGs during the Decade of Action.

Higher Education for Sustainable Development (ESD)

As the world continues to face multiple crises, including pandemics, stakeholders must prioritize Sustainable futures for young people. This means equitable access to basic Education, relevant skill building and a focus on green jobs and Green Economies.

Higher Education should work on Cross-Sectoral partnerships ensuring that children and youth have access to quality basic Education and relevant skills that can help achieve all Sustainable Development Goals.

This can happen by

- Bringing together stakeholders to discuss actions to fill gaps in Education/employment programming for Sustainable employment for young people.

- Help in Identifying Foundational Skills needed for young people to thrive in 21st century Green Economies, and to build Sustainable lifestyles, Environments, and Cities, Spotlight the role of quality basic Education, Gender Equality, and decent work in building Sustainable Cities and Communities.

- Discusses the role of all stakeholders including private sector, Civil society, Government, Business, NGOs etc to collaborate with young people and take a future forward.

- Provide a platform for young people to meaningfully engage in a dialogue with UN Member States and UN entities on transformative pathways for realizing Sustainable Development.

- Share knowledge, skills, and lessons learned in achieving the rights and well-being of youth by promoting the accelerated implementation of the 2030 Agenda and ensuring the meaningful participation and engagement of young people in policymaking and implementation.

- Present ideas and solutions -- and showcase Innovative Initiatives and individual and collective action by youth and others -- to advance the SDGs based on National, Regional and Global Experiences.

- Discuss and report on progress for the implementation of the UN Youth Strategy, Youth 2030: Working with and for Young People, and other issues related to young people including sharing information on plans for measuring and monitoring its impact at the country, regional and Global levels and considering the role that young people and youth organizations can play in the implementation of the strategy.

The Higher Education Universities Forum can provide a platform for young people to engage in a dialogue with Member States and other actors to voice their views, concerns and galvanize actions on how to transform the world into a fairer, greener and more Sustainable place guided by the Sustainable Development Goals (SDGs).

"Education is Going to be Critical for SDG Solutions."

In any theory of change, especially in the area of climate, "a piece of that has to be Education of our youth, Education of our youngest citizens — helping them understand, in a very constructive way, how the world is changing and how they can be part of having that change be something that's going to be OK for them.... That's an incredibly important challenge for everybody."

"Climate Change isn't just about warmer temperatures. It's about the potential loss of stability. In a less stable world, we're going to need a new skill: Climate Awareness. We need to be aware of the world around us. We need to bring the physical world into our lives." These are pressing issues at the intersection of Education and Climate — "Climate Change is not a future problem; Climate Change is already happening, and it affects us all,"

Let us showcase how we can and should rely on universities to teach and research while elevating the thought leadership of today's college and university students.

Higher Education should conduct research on the psychological, cultural, and political factors that influence environmental attitudes and behavior; teaches students; informs and engages the public through Environmental Journalism; and supports a Global Network of organizations seeking to build public and political will for Environmental Solutions.

Constant improvements in the availability and accessibility of Digital Technologies since the launch of the Sustainable

Development Goals (SDGs) have played an essential role in how cities, communities, governments, non-governmental agencies, and private sector firms have been able to monitor and measure their progress toward meeting the SDGs. They also have made it easier to disseminate information across those entities, facilitating cooperation among them and allowing them to be more resilient in the face of challenges such as those that have been posed by the COVID pandemic. The success of digital technologies, however, also presents ethical challenges and sometimes leads to unintended consequences. Thus, concerning how they can be positively transformed to promote Sustainable Resilience has drawn attention.

Education and investment in future generations can provide a useful and impactful approach for companies and investors to promote progress, achieve better financial outcomes, and improve ESG performance. There is growing evidence that Education is material for businesses and investors. However, a paradigm shift is needed in order to link Education and ESG more effectively, and the further development of a framework is an important first step.

To achieve these outcomes, the blueprint highlighted in the various Volumes of this Research Book - can be a vehicle for driving more active engagement and investment in Education Programs and policies, unlocking broader ESG benefits, advancing Sustainability Objectives, and Mitigating short- and long-term Corporate Risk.

The blueprint presented in this Report is an initial Framework for outlining the evidence-based aspects of Education that can have a quantifiable impact on Corporate Performance and Perception. Using it as a starting point to ensure success, a

Global Framework for Integrating ESG and Education needs to be developed.

Key Takeaway -

The Overarching goal of this Research Book is to develop a strategic Framework for Financing and Implementing Climate-Focused Education and workforce Upskilling through Public-Private Partnerships (PPPs), ensuring that SDG knowledge is curated and disseminated as a Global Public Good.

This research will contribute to:

1. Advancing Climate Literacy – by identifying effective funding mechanisms and policy models to Integrate Sustainability Education into National Curricula, Corporate Training, and Community Programs.

2. Accelerating the Green Workforce Transition – by establishing scalable upskilling initiatives in Renewable Energy, Circular Economy, and Climate-Smart Industries.

3. Enhancing ESG and SDG Impact Measurement – by defining key performance indicators (KPIs) that track the effectiveness of climate Education investments in reducing carbon footprints and fostering Sustainable Economic Growth.

4. Strengthening Public-Private Collaboration – by providing actionable insights on how Governments, Businesses, and International Organizations can co-fund and co-implement climate Education initiatives.

5. Ensuring Equitable Access to Climate Knowledge – by leveraging digital platforms, AI-driven learning tools, and

open-access repositories to make Sustainability Education widely available, particularly in underserved Regions.

The Sustainable Development Goals (SDGs) represent a universal call to action to end poverty, protect the planet, and ensure prosperity for all by 2030. Adopted by all United Nations Member States in 2015, these 17 interconnected goals with 169 specific targets provide a shared blueprint for peace and prosperity for people and the planet. Each goal addresses a specific Global challenge, ranging from inequality and Climate Change to Education and health. The SDG's aim to be achieved by 2030 to promote Sustainability, Equality and a better Quality of life for everyone worldwide.

The SDGs are not just a set of targets; they are a comprehensive framework that encourages collaboration across sectors and disciplines, emphasizing the importance of partnerships in achieving Sustainable development. For NGO professionals, understanding the SDGs is crucial as they serve as a guiding framework for project planning and implementation. By aligning their initiatives with the SDGs, NGOs can enhance their relevance and effectiveness in addressing pressing Global issues.

Moreover, the SDGs provide a common language that can facilitate collaboration with governments, businesses and other stakeholders. This alignment not only strengthens the credibility of an NGO's work but also increases its potential for funding and support from various sources that prioritize SDG-related Initiatives.

Identifying the Relevance of the SDGs to Your Proposal

How do I Ensure My Proposal Aligns with SDG's -

When developing a proposal, it is essential to identify which of the SDGs are most relevant to your project. This involves conducting a thorough analysis of the local context and understanding the specific challenges faced by the community you aim to serve. For instance, if your proposal focuses on improving access to clean water, it directly aligns with Goal 6: Clean Water and Sanitation.

By clearly articulating how your project addresses specific SDGs, you can demonstrate its significance and urgency. Additionally, consider how your proposal can contribute to multiple SDGs simultaneously. Many of the goals are interconnected; for example, improving Education (Goal 4) can lead to better economic growth (Goal 8) and reduced inequalities (Goal 10).

By highlighting these interlinkages in your proposal, you can present a more holistic approach that showcases the broader impact of your work. This not only strengthens your case but also appeals to funders who are increasingly looking for comprehensive solutions to complex problems.

Incorporating the SDGs into Your Proposal Framework

Once you have identified the relevant SDGs, the next step is to incorporate them into your proposal framework. This involves explicitly linking your project objectives, activities, and expected outcomes to specific SDG targets. For example, if your project aims to enhance women's empowerment through vocational training, you could reference Goal 5: Gender Equality and its associated targets related to women's participation in the workforce.

Incorporating the SDGs into your proposal framework also means using language that resonates with these goals. This includes adopting terminology from the SDG framework and ensuring that your objectives are SMART (Specific, Measurable, Achievable, Relevant, Time-bound). By doing so, you not only clarify your intentions but also make it easier for reviewers to see how your project aligns with Global priorities.

Furthermore, consider including a dedicated section in your proposal that explicitly outlines how each component contributes to the relevant SDGs, providing a clear roadmap for reviewers.

Ensuring the Measurable Impact of Your Proposal on the SDGs

To effectively demonstrate the impact of your proposal on the SDGs, it is vital to establish clear metrics for measurement. This involves defining key performance indicators (KPIs) that align with both your project objectives and the relevant SDG targets. For instance, if your project aims to reduce child malnutrition (Goal 2: Zero Hunger), you might track indicators such as the percentage decrease in malnutrition rates among children under five or improvements in dietary diversity.

Moreover, it is essential to develop a robust monitoring and evaluation (M&E) plan that outlines how you will collect data and assess progress over time. This plan should include baseline data collection before project implementation, regular monitoring throughout the project lifecycle, and a final evaluation to assess overall impact. By ensuring that your proposal includes a strong M&E framework, you can provide evidence of your project's effectiveness in contributing to the SDGs, which is crucial for accountability and future funding opportunities.

Engaging Stakeholders and Partners to Support the SDGs in Your Proposal

Engaging stakeholders and partners is a critical component of any successful proposal aimed at achieving the SDGs. Collaboration enhances resource sharing, knowledge exchange, and collective impact. Identify key stakeholders in your community — such as local government agencies, other NGOs, community leaders, and beneficiaries — and involve them in the proposal development process.

Their insights can help refine your project design and ensure that it addresses real needs. Additionally, consider forming partnerships with organizations that have complementary expertise or resources. For example, if your project focuses on Education (Goal 4), partnering with local schools or Educational institutions can enhance your capacity to deliver effective training programs.

Highlighting these partnerships in your proposal not only strengthens its credibility but also demonstrates a commitment to collaborative approaches that are essential for achieving Sustainable development.

Monitoring and Evaluating the Progress of your Proposal in Relation to the SDGs

Monitoring and evaluating progress is crucial for understanding how well your proposal aligns with the SDGs over time. Establishing a systematic approach to M&E allows you to track progress against defined indicators and make necessary adjustments along the way. Regularly collecting data on key performance indicators will help you assess whether you are on track to meet your objectives and contribute meaningfully to the relevant SDGs.

In addition to quantitative data collection, qualitative assessments can provide valuable insights into the experiences of beneficiaries and stakeholders. Conducting interviews or focus group discussions can help capture stories of change that illustrate how your project is making a difference. This mixed-methods approach not only enriches your understanding of impact but also provides compelling narratives that can be shared with funders and stakeholders.

Communicating the Alignment of your Proposal with the SDGs

Effective communication is essential for conveying how your proposal aligns with the SDGs. This involves crafting a compelling narrative that highlights both the urgency of the issues you are addressing and the innovative solutions you are proposing. Use clear and concise language that resonates with diverse audiences, including funders, community members, and policymakers.

Visual aids such as infographics or charts can also enhance communication by illustrating how your project contributes to specific SDG targets. Consider creating a dedicated section in your proposal that summarizes this alignment visually and textually. Additionally, leverage social media platforms and other communication channels to share updates on your project's progress in relation to the SDGs.

Engaging storytelling can help raise awareness about your work while inspiring others to take action toward Sustainable development.

Contributing to the Global Agenda through Your Proposal's Alignment with the SDGs

By aligning your proposal with the SDGs, you are not only addressing local challenges but also contributing to a Global agenda aimed at creating a more Sustainable future for all. This alignment positions your organization as part of a larger movement working toward shared goals that transcend borders. It emphasizes that local actions can have far-reaching impacts on Global issues such as Climate Change, inequality, and health crises.

Furthermore, engaging with International networks focused on the SDGs can amplify your impact. Consider participating in Global forums or initiatives that promote knowledge sharing and collaboration among NGOs working toward similar objectives. By showcasing your commitment to the SDGs through your proposal, you can inspire others in your community and beyond to join efforts toward achieving these critical goals.

Ultimately, this collective action is essential for realizing a Sustainable future where no one is left behind.

What Are the 17 SDGs? A Simple Summary of Each Goal

The Sustainable Development Goals (SDGs) consist of 17 main goals that encompass economic, social, and environmental dimensions.

The details are as follows:

1. No Poverty – Aim to eradicate poverty in all its forms, with a target to reduce by half the proportion of people living on less than $1.90 per day by 2030.

2. Zero Hunger – Focus on promoting food security, good nutrition, and Sustainable agriculture.

3. Good Health and Well-being – Reduce maternal and child mortality rates, combat epidemics, and promote mental health.

4. Quality Education – Ensure inclusive and equitable access to quality Education for all.

5. Gender Equality – Eliminate discrimination and violence against women and girls.

6. Clean Water and Sanitation – Ensure access to safe drinking water and adequate sanitation.

7. Affordable and Clean Energy – Promote the use of renewable energy and energy conservation.

8. Decent Work and Economic Growth – Promote productive employment and Sustainable economic growth.

9. Industry, Innovation, and Infrastructure – Support Sustainable industrial development and innovation.

10. Reduced Inequalities – Reduce inequalities within and among countries.

11. Sustainable Cities and Communities – Promote the development of safe, resilient, and Sustainable cities.

12. Responsible Consumption and Production – Encourage Sustainable production and consumption patterns.

13. Climate Action – Take urgent action to combat Climate Change and its impacts.

14. Life Below Water – Conserve and sustainably use ocean and marine resources.

15. Life on Land – Protect, restore, and promote the Sustainable use of terrestrial ecosystems.

16. Peace, Justice, and Strong Institutions – Foster peaceful, just, and inclusive societies.

17. Partnerships for the Goals – Strengthen Global partnerships to support Sustainable development.

Key goals, such as eradicating poverty (SDG 1), focus on raising people's income above $1.25 per day and reducing poverty in various dimensions by half by 2030. Reducing inequality (SDG 10) emphasizes addressing disparities both within and between countries. Meanwhile, tackling environmental issues (SDGs 13, 14, 15) focuses on responding to Climate Change and conserving natural resources.

Although each goal has a different focus, all 17 goals are interconnected and mutually reinforcing. For example, eradicating poverty (SDG 1) is linked to eliminating hunger (SDG 2) and promoting good health and well-being (SDG 3). Meanwhile, ensuring quality Education (SDG 4) helps reduce inequalities (SDG 10) and fosters economic growth (SDG 8).

Globally, there are examples of success in achieving the Sustainable Development Goals (SDGs), such as the reduction of extreme poverty from 36% in 1990 to 10% in 2015. In Thailand, significant progress has been made in various areas, particularly in SDG 1 (No Poverty) and SDG 4 (Quality Education), both of which have already achieved their targets. Additionally, Thailand has made advancements in clean energy (SDG 7), with key initiatives such as the People's Solar Project, which has signed power purchase agreements with 7,670 participants, with a total installed capacity of 41,791 kilowatts.

Examples of SDG Success at the Global Levels

The Nordic countries serve as a prominent example of effective implementation of the Sustainable Development Goals (SDGs). Sweden, Denmark, and Finland rank among the top three in the SDG Index rankings. Sweden has developed the concept of "SymbioCity," which integrates urban management in terms of natural resources, environment, and energy in a holistic manner. Examples include utilizing excess heat from industries for household use and converting waste and wastewater into biogas. Denmark has achieved significant success in waste management, recycling up to 60% of its waste and generating 95% of its electricity from waste incineration. A key issue is the lack of legal measures to support the initiative, as well as the need to raise public awareness.

A crucial lesson from implementing the Sustainable Development Goals (SDGs) is the necessity of policy integration and multi-stakeholder participation. The level of government commitment is a significant factor influencing SDG Index scores. Countries ranking at the top typically have well-defined plans for SDG implementation.

Citizens can contribute to the SDGs in various ways, such as adopting Sustainable daily habits, reducing the use of single-use plastics, using energy efficiently, and supporting eco-friendly products and services. Additionally, staying informed about sustainability issues and participating in community activities that promote the SDGs are other ways individuals can help drive Sustainable Development Goals forward.

Measurement and Monitoring of SDG Progress

The measurement and tracking of Sustainable Development Goals (SDGs) progress is a crucial process in advancing Sustainable development objectives. This involves assessment methods at both National and Global levels.

At the Global level, the United Nations has developed the SDG Tracker, a key tool for monitoring progress across all 17 SDGs. This tool utilizes interactive data visualization to compile information from various sources, including the United Nations, the World Bank, and the World Health Organization (WHO).

The evaluation is based on UN indicators and National strategies to assess the development status of each sub-goal.

Key indicators for each Goal vary, such as:

- SDG 1 (No Poverty): The proportion of the population living on less than $1.90 per day.

- SDG 4 (Quality Education): Enrolment rates in primary and secondary Education.

- SDG 13 (Climate Action): The volume of greenhouse gas emissions.

International organizations play a crucial role in monitoring the progress of the Sustainable Development Goals (SDGs). The United Nations (UN) sets the indicator framework and compiles data from member states. The World Bank supports data collection and economic analysis. Meanwhile, National governments are responsible for collecting data, reporting progress, and submitting Voluntary National Reviews (VNRs) to the High-Level Political Forum (HLPF).

However, measuring and tracking the progress of the Sustainable Development Goals (SDGs) still face several challenges, including:

1. Incomplete data, particularly in developing countries.

2. Variations in data collection methods across countries, making comparisons difficult.

3. Limited capacity for in-depth data analysis.

4. Delays in reporting, which can result in outdated information that does not reflect the current situation.

Addressing these challenges requires International cooperation, capacity building in statistical analysis, and the use of modern technology for data collection and analysis to ensure more effective and accurate SDG monitoring.

How can we Contribute to the SDGs?

Sustainable consumption is one of the key ways in which the general public can support the Sustainable Development Goals (SDGs), particularly Goal 12, which focuses on responsible consumption and production. People can adjust their consumption habits by considering the value of goods and services and their environmental impact. This includes buying and consuming only what is necessary, reducing the use of non-biodegradable or single-use packaging, and sorting waste to facilitate proper disposal and recycling.

Supporting Sustainable organizations and businesses is another way individuals can contribute. This can be done by choosing to support businesses that utilize clean or renewable energy in their production processes, purchasing products from stores that use biodegradable and reusable materials, and using energy-efficient and environmentally friendly transportation services.

The business sector plays a crucial role in driving the Sustainable Development Goals (SDGs) by leveraging its core capabilities and expertise to foster engagement and community development. Businesses can integrate SDGs into their strategies and operations, particularly multiNational corporations and large enterprises, which should adopt Sustainable practices and incorporate sustainability data into their corporate reporting cycles.

Technology and innovation are key enablers in achieving SDGs, with Artificial Intelligence (AI) playing a particularly significant role in solving complex problems and navigating an unpredictable future. Examples of AI applications supporting SDGs include Rewire, which combats online hate speech; ASM Spotter, which monitors illegal mining activities; and NASA Harvest, which provides data to enhance food security.

The future of SDGs faces significant challenges, particularly in Environmental Issues and Inequality. Achieving the targets by 2030 requires Collaboration from all sectors, including Government, Private enterprises, Civil Society, and the general public. A key challenge is Integrating policies and fostering genuine participation, alongside advancing Technology and Innovation to accelerate progress toward SDGs within the set timeframe.

The Future of SDGs: Directions and Challenges Ahead

The Sustainable Development Goals (SDGs) are facing significant challenges in achieving their targets by 2030, particularly in environmental issues and inequality. According to the SDG Index 2024 report, only 16% of the SDG sub-targets are projected to be met Globally by 2030, while 84% are either facing limitations or experiencing a reversal in progress.

Climate Change remains a major challenge affecting multiple SDG targets, particularly SDG 13 (Climate Action), which continues to face difficulties. Greenhouse gas emissions are still rising, leading to more severe natural disasters that threaten food Security (SDG 2) and Public Health (SDG 3).

Economic and social conflicts pose significant challenges to achieving the Sustainable Development Goals (SDGs), particularly SDG 10 (Reducing Inequality) and SDG 16 (Peace, Justice, and Strong Institutions), both of which remain highly challenging. The COVID-19 pandemic has further exacerbated Economic and Social Inequalities.

However, there are promising trends in driving SDGs forward in the future, such as:

1. The use of technology and innovation, particularly Artificial Intelligence (AI), to address complex problems and navigate an unpredictable future.

2. The integration of SDGs into National policies and planning, especially in countries where Governments demonstrate strong commitment.

3. The increasing role of the Private Sector in advancing SDGs by embedding Sustainability Goals into corporate strategies and operations.

4. Raising Public Awareness and participation through behavioural changes in daily life, such as adopting Sustainable consumption practices.

SDGs are a matter for everyone, as they encompass all Dimensions of Development — Economic, Social, and Environmental — under the principle of "leaving no one behind." Achieving the SDGs will lead to a more Sustainable, Equitable world with a better quality of life for all. Therefore, prioritizing the SDGs is an investment in our future and that of the next generations. The participation of all sectors, from policymaking to daily actions, will be key to driving the SDGs toward success by 2030.

Chapter 2

Conversion of UN's SDG's into a Reality : The Strategies and Operational Mechanisms for the Remaining Five Year Period 2026 -2030

"From Commitment to Impact: Turning the UN SDGs into Reality"

The Sustainable Development Goals (SDGs) represent a shared Global blueprint to secure a just, inclusive, and resilient future by 2030. Converting the SDGs from aspirational frameworks into measurable realities hinges on aligning policies, partnerships, and investments with clear strategies and operational mechanisms. This section outlines the practical pathways, innovations, and governance models necessary to move from commitment to delivery.

Yet with less than five years remaining, the time for reflection has passed — what is now required is urgent, collective action. Converting the SDGs into reality demands that governments embed sustainability into policy and governance, businesses align innovation and investment with impact, civil society mobilize communities for change, academia provide evidence-based solutions, and individuals champion responsible choices. Real progress lies in breaking down silos and fostering integrated, locally grounded strategies that translate Global ambition into tangible outcomes. This section explores the mechanisms, partnerships, and pathways required to transform the SDGs from Global pledges into real-world progress for all.

Given that we are only five years away from 2030, reaching SDG 1 will require radical acceleration.

Here's a realistic and action-focused guideline to drive progress on **SDG 1** (End Poverty in All Its Forms Everywhere) between 2025 and 2030:

1. Scale Up Direct Social Protection Systems

- Immediate Action:

  o Expand universal social protection floors (cash transfers, food security programs, child benefits, old-age pensions) in all countries, especially low- and middle-income nations.

- How:

  o Use innovative financing (solidarity taxes, debt swaps for SDGs, blended finance models) to fund these systems sustainably.

- Goal by 2026:

  o 100% coverage of the most vulnerable populations with basic income security and access to essential services.

2. Prioritize Pro-Poor Economic Recovery and Job Creation

- Immediate Action:

  o Design all National recovery plans to be explicitly pro-poor, focusing on job-intensive sectors (e.g., agriculture, Sustainable manufacturing, construction, local services).

- How:

  o Create "green economy jobs" targeting rural areas, women, youth, and displaced communities.

- Goal by 2027:

    - Cut unemployment among vulnerable populations by at least 50%, and create millions of resilient livelihoods.

3. Invest Massively in Rural Development and Basic Infrastructure

- Immediate Action:

    - Focus infrastructure spending on rural roads, electrification, clean water access, digital inclusion, and healthcare systems.

- How:

    - Channel public-private investments into rural economies through inclusive finance platforms and SDG impact bonds.

- Goal by 2027:

    - Connect 90% of rural communities to basic infrastructure and services, reducing multidimensional poverty.

4. Ensure Universal Access to Education, Healthcare, and Financial Services

- Immediate Action:

    - Make free, quality Education, basic healthcare, and microfinance services universally accessible.

- How:

    - Deploy mobile health units, digital learning platforms, and mobile banking solutions into underserved areas.

- Goal by 2028:

    - All people living in extreme poverty have access to Education, health, and financial services.

5. Strengthen Climate Resilience for the Poor

- Immediate Action:

    - Implement climate adaptation programs that protect the livelihoods of farmers, fishermen, indigenous peoples, and vulnerable urban populations.

- How:

    - Invest in disaster risk reduction, climate-smart agriculture, micro-insurance programs, and resilient infrastructure.

- Goal by 2028:

    - Ensure that communities most vulnerable to climate shocks are actively participating in resilience-building initiatives.

6. Tackle Systemic Inequalities and Structural Barriers

- Immediate Action:

    - Pass and enforce anti-discrimination, pro-inclusion laws that protect marginalized groups.

    - Promote decent work standards, land rights for women, fair wages, and secure tenure for informal settlements.

- Goal by 2029:

    - Remove legal and social barriers that trap communities in poverty.

7. Enhance Data Systems to Target and Track Poverty Reduction

- Immediate Action:
  - Build real-time poverty tracking platforms using big data, mobile surveys, and AI-based predictive analytics.
- How:
  - Disaggregate data by income, gender, age, disability, ethnicity, and geographic location to leave no one behind.
- Goal by 2026:
  - All countries have up-to-date poverty data that informs targeted policy action.

In Summary: Key Accelerators for SDG 1 (No Poverty)

Priority	Goal by 2030
Universal social protection coverage	100% basic income and services for the poor
Pro-poor economic growth & green jobs	Halve unemployment among vulnerable groups
Rural infrastructure & connectivity	90% rural access to roads, electricity, and water
Universal access to Education & finance	Education, healthcare, financial services for all
Climate resilience for the poor	Protect livelihoods from climate shocks
Dismantle systemic inequalities	Equal rights, fair access, and inclusion
Data-driven poverty targeting	Real-time poverty tracking systems operational

Tone for 2025–2030:

Urgent, Inclusive, Pro-Poor, Resilient, and Data-Driven.

II. Strategies and Operational Mechanisms to Reach SDG 2 by 2030

SDG 2: Zero Hunger — another absolutely critical goal, especially in today's context of rising food insecurity, climate shocks, and conflict-driven crises.

Since we have only five years left, the strategies must be bold, integrated, and accelerated.

Here's a clear and practical guide for strategies and operational mechanisms to reach SDG 2: Zero Hunger by 2030:

"This roadmap defines an urgent, technology-driven, and nutrition-focused strategy to eliminate hunger and build resilient, Sustainable food systems by 2030. Collaboration, innovation, and inclusive rural development will be key to ending hunger in our lifetime."

A. Strategies (What Needs to Be Done)

1.Transform Food Systems Toward Sustainability and Resilience

Shift from just increasing yields to building Sustainable, inclusive, and climate-resilient food systems.

Promote climate-smart agriculture, agroecology, regenerative farming, and circular food economies.

Diversify crops to include nutrient-rich and climate-resilient varieties (e.g., millets, legumes, indigenous crops).

Goal: Ensure that all National food systems are aligned with both nutrition outcomes and climate resilience by 2027.

2. Prioritize Nutrition-Sensitive Approaches

Integrate nutrition into all agricultural and food policies — not just quantity, but quality.

Strengthen maternal and child nutrition programs, especially during the critical first 1,000 days (pregnancy to age 2).

Implement food fortification strategies (iodine, iron, folic acid) at mass scale.

Goal: End all forms of malnutrition (undernutrition, stunting, wasting, micronutrient deficiencies) by 2030.

3. Empower Smallholder Farmers and Rural Producers

Support small-scale farmers with access to finance, insurance, digital platforms, resilient seeds, and Sustainable techniques.

Improve rural infrastructure (irrigation, roads, storage) and secure fair prices for smallholders.

Promote land rights for women farmers, youth engagement, and indigenous community empowerment.

Goal: Double the productivity and incomes of smallholder farmers by 2028.

4. Build Social Protection and Emergency Food Systems

Expand shock-responsive food safety nets (cash transfers, food vouchers, school meals programs) in fragile and conflict-prone regions.

Establish Global and regional food reserves to quickly respond to famines, droughts, or displacement crises.

Goal: Achieve universal access to social protection systems that guarantee food security by 2027.

5. Reduce Food Loss and Waste by Half

Strengthen value chain infrastructure (cold storage, better logistics) to reduce post-harvest losses.

Launch National campaigns to cut food waste at the retail and consumer levels.

Engage private sector in circular economy models for food (recycling, upcycling, redistribution).

Goal: Halve Global food loss and waste by 2028.

B. Operational Mechanisms (How to Deliver the Strategies)

1. Multi-Stakeholder National Food Action Plans

- Each country must develop and implement a National Food Systems Transformation Roadmap aligned with SDG 2.

- Include ministries of agriculture, health, Education, finance, private sector, farmers' organizations, and civil society.

Operational Timeline: By 2025, every country should have a Food Systems Transformation Plan.

2. Scaling Digital Agriculture and Innovation

- Use AI, IoT, satellite data, and mobile technology to improve:

    o Weather forecasting

    o Early warning systems

    o Digital marketplaces (farmers to consumers)

    o Smart irrigation and precision farming

- Support open-access digital agriculture platforms for smallholders.

Operational Timeline: Digital extension services reaching 80% of small farmers by 2027.

3. Blended Financing for Agriculture and Nutrition Programs

- Mobilize public-private investments using blended finance models (grants + impact investment) to support:

    o Smallholder credit systems

    o Agro-processing businesses

    o Nutritious food production

Create dedicated "Zero Hunger Impact Funds" at National and regional levels.

Operational Timeline: 30% increase in agricultural and food security investment flows by 2026.

4. Strengthening Regional and Global Collaboration

- Activate regional alliances like the African Union's Comprehensive Africa Agriculture Development

Programme (CAADP) or ASEAN's Food Security Framework.

- Promote south-south cooperation for knowledge transfer and resilience building.

Operational Timeline: All regions have active food security cooperation platforms by 2026.

5. Robust Monitoring, Accountability, and Adaptation Systems

- Establish real-time, open-access food security dashboards at the National and Global levels (using WFP, FAO, WHO data).

- Set mandatory SDG 2 reporting standards for governments and corporations engaged in food systems.

- Adapt programs continuously based on evidence and emerging risks (climate, conflict, pandemics).

Operational Timeline: Real-time monitoring of food insecurity in every country by 2026.

In Summary: Fast-Track Priorities for SDG 2

Priority	Goal by 2030
Resilient food systems	Climate-smart, nutrition-focused agriculture
End malnutrition	Eliminate stunting, wasting, micronutrient deficiencies
Empower smallholder farmers	Double productivity and incomes
Expand social protection	Food security for the vulnerable

Reduce food loss and waste	Cut by 50% Globally
Accelerate digital innovation	80% farmers reached by tech platforms
Strengthen Global partnerships	Regional food security frameworks active

Tone for 2025–2030:

Transformative, Resilient, Nutrition-Focused, Digital-First, Inclusive.

Visual Roadmap: Reaching SDG 2(Zero Hunger) by 2030

2025: Foundation Year – National and Global Food Action Plans

- Launch National Food Systems Transformation Plans (multi-stakeholder driven).

- Expand emergency food assistance programs for the most vulnerable populations.

- Mobilize Zero Hunger Impact Funds (using blended finance models).

2026: Technology and Resilience Expansion

- Scale digital agriculture solutions (AI, IoT, smart irrigation, mobile extension services).

- Strengthen smallholder access to finance, seeds, markets, and climate-resilient farming tools.

- Establish real-time National food security monitoring dashboards.

2027: Nutrition Revolution and Rural Infrastructure Boost

- Integrate nutrition-sensitive agriculture into National policies and Education systems.

- Expand maternal, child nutrition, and school meals programs.

- Complete critical rural infrastructure projects (roads, electrification, cold storage).

2028: Halving Food Loss, Empowering Farmers, Strengthening Climate Adaptation

- Launch major National food loss and waste reduction campaigns (retail, consumer, logistics).

- Double smallholder productivity and incomes through fair trade policies, cooperatives, and value chain support.

- Implement large-scale climate adaptation programs (insurance, early warning, resilient crops).

2029: Consolidation of Systems and Global Knowledge Sharing

- Strengthen regional and Global cooperation frameworks for food security.

- Document and share successful National models of Sustainable food systems transformation.

- Align final five-year reviews with SDG 2 targets Globally.

2030: Achievement of Zero Hunger Goal

- Universal access to safe, nutritious, and sufficient food for all people, year-round.

- Eradication of stunting, wasting, and severe food insecurity worldwide.

- Sustainable food systems fully operational and climate-resilient.

Strategies and Operational Mechanisms to Reach SDG 3 (Good Health and Well-Being) by 2030

A. Strategies (What Needs to Be Done)

1. Achieve Universal Health Coverage (UHC) and Financial Protection

- Expand access to affordable and quality healthcare services for all, regardless of income, gender, or location.

- Eliminate out-of-pocket payments that push people into poverty.

- Implement publicly financed health systems with strong risk pooling.

Goal: By 2027, at least 80% of each country's population should have access to essential health services.

2. Strengthen Primary Health Care Systems

- Invest in primary healthcare (PHC) as the frontline of the health system.

- Ensure availability of basic medicines, vaccines, diagnostics, and trained healthcare workers at the community level.

- Integrate mental health services into PHC.

Goal: By 2026, PHC must cover preventive, promotive, curative, rehabilitative, and palliative services.

3. Prioritize Maternal, Newborn, Child, and Adolescent Health

- Scale up programs that ensure safe pregnancies, childbirth, and neonatal care.

- Universal access to immunizations, nutrition programs, and adolescent reproductive health Education.

- Eliminate preventable deaths of mothers and children.

Goal: By 2027, reduce maternal mortality to less than 70 per 100,000 live births Globally.

4. Tackle Non-Communicable Diseases (NCDs) and Mental Health

- Implement National strategies for prevention and management of cardiovascular diseases, diabetes, cancers, and respiratory diseases.

- Promote lifestyle changes: reduce tobacco use, promote healthy diets, increase physical activity.

- Strengthen mental health promotion and suicide prevention services.

Goal: By 2028, achieve a 30% reduction in premature mortality from NCDs.

5. Prepare for and Respond to Health Emergencies

- Strengthen pandemic preparedness systems, resilient supply chains, and emergency response capacity.

- Build early warning systems using AI, satellite data, and mobile health technologies.

- Maintain routine immunization and health services during crises.

Goal: By 2026, all countries have fully operational, WHO-aligned pandemic preparedness plans.

B. Operational Mechanisms (How to Deliver the Strategies)

1. Scale Public Health Investments and Innovative Financing

- Increase public health expenditure to at least 5% of GDP.

- Use blended financing models: domestic budgets + International aid + private sector investment (e.g., health impact bonds).

- Mobilize climate-health financing for environmental determinants of health (air quality, heatwaves, clean water).

Operational Goal: By 2025, National health budgets aligned with SDG 3 financing targets.

2. Expand Digital Health Innovations

- Deploy telemedicine, AI-based diagnostics, mobile health (mHealth) apps, and electronic health records.

- Strengthen digital infrastructure in rural and underserved communities.

- Launch open-source digital platforms to democratize access to healthcare information.

Operational Goal: By 2027, digital health services accessible to at least 70% of rural and remote populations.

3. Build the Health Workforce of the Future

- Train, retain, and fairly compensate healthcare workers — especially in underserved areas.

- Invest in community health worker programs, midwifery training, and mental health counseling certifications.

- Strengthen cross-border collaboration for health worker mobility in regions with shortages.

Operational Goal: By 2027, an additional 18 million health workers Globally trained and deployed (WHO target).

4. Strengthen Health Governance, Accountability, and Equity

- Embed health equity into all National policies ("Health in All Policies" approach).

- Create community-driven health accountability mechanisms (local monitoring, citizen reporting).

- Disaggregate health data by gender, income, age, geography, and ethnicity.

Operational Goal: By 2026, equity-focused health reporting frameworks operational in all countries.

5. Strengthen Multilateral and Global Health Partnerships

- Boost support for WHO, Gavi (the Vaccine Alliance), Global Fund, CEPI (Coalition for Epidemic Preparedness Innovations).

- Create regional pandemic response hubs in Africa, Asia, and Latin America.

- Scale Global vaccine and essential medicine access

programs (e.g., COVAX, ACT Accelerator).

Operational Goal: By 2026, coordinated Global systems for vaccine equity and emergency response fully functional.

In Summary: Fast-Track Priorities for SDG 3

Priority	Goal by 2030
Universal Health Coverage (UHC)	100% essential services access for all
Primary Health Care Strengthening	Fully operational PHC networks worldwide
Maternal and Child Health	End preventable maternal and newborn deaths
Fight NCDs and Promote Mental Health	30% reduction in premature deaths from NCDs
Emergency Preparedness	Pandemic readiness in all countries
Digital Health Revolution	Telemedicine and AI-based health access Globally

Tone for 2025–2030:

Equitable, Resilient, Prevention-Focused, Technology-Enabled, Community-Driven.

Visual Roadmap: Reaching SDG 3 (Good Health and Well-Being) by 2030

[Timeline Layout: Horizontal timeline from 2025 to 2030, milestones at each year]

2025: Foundation Year – Universal Access and Financing Boost

- Scale up National Universal Health Coverage (UHC) plans with strong financial protection.

- Expand public health budgets to at least 5% of GDP.

- Launch health workforce recruitment drives (community health workers, midwives, digital health specialists).

2026: Strengthening Primary Health Care and Emergency Preparedness

- Modernize Primary Health Care (PHC) systems with integrated mental health services.

- Deploy digital health platforms in rural and underserved areas.

- Implement pandemic preparedness frameworks at National and regional levels.

2027: Expanding NCDs and Mental Health Programs

- Scale National campaigns on healthy lifestyles (tobacco control, physical activity, nutrition).

- Launch mental health integration programs at PHC centers.

- Strengthen school-based health services for children and adolescents.

2028: Equity, Innovation, and Resilience Focus

- Fully operationalize health equity frameworks across all countries.

- Achieve 70%+ coverage for digital health access in rural and marginalized communities.

- Boost climate-resilient healthcare infrastructure (e.g., solar-powered clinics).

2029: Global Health System Strengthening and Final Alignment

- Regional emergency response hubs operational for pandemic and health emergency response.

- Universal access to essential medicines, vaccines, and diagnostics guaranteed.

- Global best practices and innovations shared systematically across countries.

2030: Achievement of SDG 3 Goals

- Universal Health Coverage achieved — no one left behind.

- End preventable maternal, newborn, and child deaths.

- Reduce premature mortality from NCDs by one-third.

- Strong, resilient, equitable health systems in every country.

Strategies and Operational Mechanisms for Achieving SDG 4 by 2030

(Goal: Ensure inclusive, equitable, and quality Education and promote lifelong learning for all)

Strategies and Operational Mechanisms for Achieving SDG 4 by 2030

(Goal: Ensure inclusive, equitable, and quality Education and promote lifelong learning for all)

A. Strategies (What Needs to Be Done)

1. Make Inclusive and Equitable Education Mandatory and Universal

- Focus on universal access to free, quality primary and secondary Education, with targeted efforts in underserved areas (rural, displaced, marginalized communities).

- Expand early childhood Education programs, especially in low-income countries.

Goal by 2026: Full free access to basic Education Globally.

2. Prioritize Digital and Blended Learning Models

- Invest in EdTech solutions, including mobile learning, online platforms, and remote teaching tools.

- Promote hybrid learning models (in-person + digital) to make Education resilient against future disruptions.

Goal by 2027: 80% of schools Globally equipped for digital learning.

3. Accelerate Teacher Training, Recruitment, and Retention

- Massively scale up teacher recruitment to address Global teacher shortages, especially for STEM and sustainability subjects.

- Implement continuous professional development (CPD) programs focused on digital skills, SDGs, climate Education, and inclusive pedagogy.

Goal by 2027: Train 69 million teachers needed for universal Education (UNESCO target).

4. Integrate SDG, Climate, and Future Skills into Curricula

- Update National curricula to include Climate Change Education, sustainability literacy, civic engagement, and digital competencies.

- Foster skills for the green economy, entrepreneurship, critical thinking, and Global citizenship.

Goal by 2026: Climate and SDG Education included in all National curricula.

5. Promote Lifelong Learning and Skills for Employment

- Build pathways for youth and adults to acquire vocational, technical, and digital skills aligned with emerging industries.

- Strengthen access to Technical and Vocational Education and Training (TVET) and second-chance Education programs.

Goal by 2028: All adults have pathways to reskill or upskill for the future economy.

B. Operational Mechanisms (How to Deliver the Strategies)

1. Develop National SDG 4 Action Plans and Legal Frameworks

- Governments must urgently finalize and adopt National Education acceleration strategies based on SDG 4 benchmarks.

- Pass laws ensuring compulsory, free, quality Education for at least 12 years.

Operational Timeline: All countries have SDG 4 implementation laws and plans by 2025.

2. Mobilize Sustainable Financing for Education

- Increase domestic Education budgets to at least 4-6% of GDP and 15-20% of total public expenditure (UNESCO recommendation).

- Attract private sector investments through public-private partnerships (PPPs) and Education Impact Bonds.

- Expand Global Education funds (e.g., Global Partnership for Education, Education Cannot Wait).

Operational Timeline: 30% increase in Education financing flows Globally by 2026.

3. Strengthen Public-Private Partnerships (PPPs) in Education Delivery

- Leverage private innovation and funding for EdTech expansion, teacher training, infrastructure building, and skills development programs.

- Formalize partnerships between governments, corporations, NGOs, and universities.

Operational Timeline: PPPs operational in Education systems in all countries by 2026.

4. Target Equity and Inclusion Measures

- Launch special initiatives targeting girls' Education, Education for children with disabilities, refugees, indigenous populations, and rural youth.

- Expand conditional cash transfer programs (school meal incentives, transportation subsidies) to boost enrolment and completion.

Operational Timeline: Gender parity and significant reduction in exclusion rates achieved by 2027.

5. Implement Robust Monitoring, Data, and Accountability Systems

- Use real-time Education monitoring systems (big data, AI analytics) to track learning outcomes, enrolment rates, teacher gaps, and equity indicators.

- Establish transparent National and Global reporting on SDG 4 progress every year.

Operational Timeline: Real-time SDG 4 Education dashboards operational Globally by 2026.

In Summary: Fast-Track Priorities for SDG 4 (Quality Education)

Priority Area	Goal by 2030
Free, inclusive basic Education	100% Global access to primary and secondary Education
Digital and blended learning	80% schools digitally connected
Teacher recruitment and training	69 million teachers trained and deployed
Updated curriculum for SDGs/Climate	SDG literacy universal in Education
Skills for employment and lifelong learning	Vocational and digital skills available for all
Equity and inclusion initiatives	No gender gap, no marginalized groups left behind
Strong financing and accountability	Sustainable Education financing systems in place

Tone for 2025–2030:

Urgent, Inclusive, Technology-Driven, Future-Ready, Equity-Focused, Action-Oriented.

Visual Roadmap: Reaching SDG 4 Targets by 2030

Timeline Layout:

POLICY

2025: Foundation Year – Immediate Policy and Financing Action

- Mandate SDG and climate Education in National curricula (K-12, higher ed, vocational).

- Launch National and regional Education Acceleration Funds (using public and private finance).

- Establish public-private partnerships (PPPs) focused on Education infrastructure and teacher upskilling.

TECHNOLOGY

2026: Technology Expansion and Curriculum Overhaul

- Deploy AI, VR, and mobile learning technologies to rural, underserved, and marginalized communities.

- Roll out updated curricula integrating sustainability, digital skills, and green economy competencies.

- Introduce teacher certification programs on climate literacy and digital Education tools.

WORKFORCE

2027: Mass Green Workforce Upskilling and Access Equity

- Scale workforce training programs for green jobs

(renewables, circular economy, Sustainable agriculture).

- Ensure gender parity and inclusive enrolment (especially for girls, indigenous communities, refugees).

- Strengthen digital Education networks through public-private investments in connectivity.

MONITORING

2028: Monitoring, Evaluation, and Adaptive Learning Systems

- Launch National SDG 4 real-time monitoring dashboards using AI and big data.

- Start linking Education outcomes with employment, environmental, and social equity indicators.

- Adapt programs based on real-time feedback: improving curriculum delivery, funding, and outreach strategies.

BEST PRACTICES

2029: Full System Integration and Global Best Practices

- Consolidate climate and SDG literacy as a core competency in all Education sectors.

- Share National best practices Globally via UN platforms and Global partnerships.

- Strengthen partnerships with ESG investors to sustain long-term funding and innovation in Education.

ACHIEVEMENT

2030: Achievement and Continuous Learning Commitment

- Universal access to quality, inclusive, and SDG-aligned

Education achieved.

- Strong green economy workforce pipeline established.

- Climate literacy mainstreamed Globally across all Education levels.

- Sustainability learning embedded into lifelong learning pathways for all.

Strategies and Operational Mechanisms to Achieve SDG 5: Gender Equality by 2030

A. Strategies (What Needs to Be Done)

1. Legally Guarantee Equal Rights for Women and Girls

- Enact and enforce laws guaranteeing equal rights to economic resources, inheritance, property ownership, Education, political participation, and employment.

- Strengthen laws against gender-based violence, workplace discrimination, and child marriage.

Goal: By 2026, eliminate discriminatory laws in all countries.

2. End Gender-Based Violence (GBV) in All Forms

- Implement National action plans to prevent and respond to all forms of GBV (domestic violence, sexual harassment, trafficking, harmful practices).

- Expand access to survivor-centered services (legal, psychological, shelter, healthcare).

- Make public spaces, transport, and schools safe for women and girls.

Goal: By 2027, drastically reduce rates of GBV, with survivor support services available everywhere.

3. Promote Equal Participation in Leadership and Decision-Making

- Introduce gender quotas or targets for political offices, corporate leadership, and public administration.

- Support mentorship and leadership development programs for women and girls.

- Eliminate barriers to women's participation in peacebuilding, climate action, and economic decision-making.

Goal: By 2028, achieve at least 50% women's representation in leadership across all sectors.

4. Ensure Equal Access to Education and Economic Opportunities

- Eliminate gender gaps in access to primary, secondary, and higher Education.

- Promote STEM Education and entrepreneurship programs for women and girls.

- Facilitate access to credit, land, skills training, and digital tools for women entrepreneurs.

Goal: By 2027, gender parity in Education and economic participation Globally.

5. Recognize and Redistribute Unpaid Care and Domestic Work

- Implement National care policies (paid parental leave, childcare services, eldercare) to reduce and redistribute unpaid work.

- Include care economy investments in public budgets and National employment strategies.

Goal: By 2026, establish care systems and policies in all countries.

B. Operational Mechanisms (How to Deliver the Strategies)

1. Legislative Reform and Policy Frameworks

- Governments must pass and implement gender-equal laws aligned with CEDAW (Convention on the Elimination of All Forms of Discrimination Against Women) and SDG 5 targets.

- Create National Gender Equality Action Plans with clear budgets and accountability mechanisms.

Operational Timeline: Gender-responsive legal frameworks adopted by all countries by 2025.

2. Sustainable Financing for Gender Equality

- Allocate at least 5–10% of National budgets to gender equality programs.

- Create Gender Equality Funds (public-private-philanthropic partnerships) to finance women's economic empowerment, GBV prevention, and leadership development.

Operational Timeline: Dedicated gender equality financing mechanisms operational by 2026.

3. Multi-Sector Collaboration and Public-Private Partnerships

- Engage governments, businesses, civil society, and

International organizations in coordinated gender equality programs.

- Launch corporate gender equality pledges, workplace audits, and ESG-linked incentives for gender equity performance.

Operational Timeline: PPP-driven gender equality initiatives active in all regions by 2026.

4. Expand Data Systems and Gender-Disaggregated Monitoring

- Build National data systems that disaggregate data by gender, age, location, disability, income, and ethnicity.
- Regularly track and publish gender equality progress reports linked to SDG 5 indicators.

Operational Timeline: Gender-responsive National statistical systems operational Globally by 2027.

5. Accelerate Grassroots Movements and Community Mobilization

- Support women's organizations, youth networks, and feminist movements to lead advocacy, Education, and policy campaigns.
- Invest in community-driven approaches for cultural change toward gender equality.

Operational Timeline: Grassroots gender equality movements strengthened in every country by 2026.

In Summary: Fast-Track Priorities for SDG 5

Priority Area	Goal by 2030
Legal Rights and Anti-Discrimination	Equal legal status for women and men
Ending Gender-Based Violence	Comprehensive GBV prevention and survivor services
Women's Leadership and Representation	50% representation in politics, business, public life
Education and Economic Empowerment	Full gender parity in Education, entrepreneurship
Recognition of Care Work	National policies valuing and redistributing unpaid work
Data and Accountability Systems	Gender-disaggregated monitoring systems Globally

Visual Roadmap: Reaching SDG 5 (Gender Equality) Targets by 2030

[Timeline Layout: Horizontal format — milestones for each year from 2025 to 2030]

2025: Foundation Year – Legal Reforms and National Action Plans

- Adopt comprehensive gender equality laws (aligned with CEDAW and SDG 5).

- Launch National Gender Equality Action Plans with clear funding commitments.

- Prioritize removal of discriminatory legal barriers to women's rights (inheritance, employment, land ownership, political participation).

2026: Care Economy and Violence Prevention Systems Expansion

- Establish National care systems (parental leave policies, affordable childcare, eldercare support).

- Fully operationalize survivor-centered GBV response systems (hotlines, shelters, legal aid).

- Expand gender-responsive budgets in all sectors (health, Education, employment, infrastructure).

2027: Leadership, Education, and Economic Parity Focus

- Achieve gender parity in Education (at all levels, including STEM fields).

- Introduce leadership quotas (50% minimum women representation in politics and corporations).

- Launch large-scale women entrepreneurship programs with access to finance, digital tools, and mentorship.

2028: Data Revolution and Systemic Inclusion Expansion

- Fully operational gender-disaggregated National data systems (income, leadership, health, Education, violence).

- Strengthen workplace gender audits and enforce corporate gender equality standards.

- Expand rural, indigenous, refugee women's access to Education, health, land rights, and technology.

2029: Global Consolidation of Best Practices and Final Acceleration Push

- Share successful models Globally through UN platforms,

regional forums, and SDG summits.

- Scale community-driven gender equality movements (grassroots leadership in all regions).

- Align final National reviews with SDG 5 achievement frameworks.

2030: Achievement of Gender Equality Goals

- Full legal equality achieved.

- End of gender-based violence as a systemic issue.

- Equal leadership representation across politics, business, and civil society.

- Recognition and redistribution of unpaid care work Globally.

- Sustainable gender-responsive systems embedded into governance, economy, and society.

Strategies and Operational Mechanisms to Achieve SDG 6: Clean Water and Sanitation by 2030

"This roadmap offers a transformative plan to achieve SDG 6 by 2030 — ensuring universal access to clean water and sanitation through smart investments, resilient infrastructure, innovation, and community-driven governance. Water for all, by all."

A. Strategies (What Needs to Be Done)

1. Universal Access to Safe Drinking Water and Sanitation Services

- Scale up investment in water supply infrastructure — wells, pipelines, reservoirs, purification plants.

- Build sanitation systems (toilets, sewerage, waste treatment) for rural, urban, and displaced populations.

- Focus on affordability and equitable access, especially for low-income and marginalized communities.

Goal: By 2027, provide safely managed water and sanitation to all people.

2. Improve Water Quality and Reduce Pollution

- Strictly regulate industrial wastewater, agricultural runoff, and urban sewage discharge.

- Promote wastewater treatment and reuse technologies.

- Implement nature-based solutions (e.g., wetlands restoration, watershed protection) to naturally purify water.

Goal: By 2026, halve the proportion of untreated wastewater Globally.

3. Strengthen Water Resource Management and Efficiency

- Develop Integrated Water Resources Management (IWRM) systems at the National and regional levels.

- Promote efficient irrigation systems (drip, sprinkler) and water-saving technologies.

- Support community-led water governance models, empowering local stakeholders.

Goal: By 2027, implement IWRM plans in 100% of countries.

4. Build Climate Resilient Water and Sanitation Infrastructure

- Design infrastructure to withstand climate risks: droughts, floods, rising sea levels, and extreme weather.

- Prioritize green infrastructure solutions (e.g., rainwater harvesting, permeable urban surfaces).

Goal: By 2028, ensure all new water infrastructure is climate resilient.

5. Protect and Restore Water-Related Ecosystems

- Rehabilitate rivers, lakes, wetlands, aquifers, and watersheds.

- Enforce strict protection measures for critical water ecosystems.

- Link water ecosystem health to climate adaptation and biodiversity goals.

Goal: By 2027, significant Global progress in restoring degraded water ecosystems.

B. Operational Mechanisms (How to Deliver the Strategies)

1. Scale Up Investment and Innovative Financing for Water Systems

- Increase public investment in water and sanitation to at least 1% of GDP.

- Mobilize blended finance models: public budgets, private sector contributions, climate funds, and development aid.

- Create Water Investment Funds to support National projects and regional transboundary programs.

Operational Timeline: Blended financing frameworks operational Globally by 2026.

2. Strengthen Water Governance and Cross-Sector Coordination

- Establish National water authorities with clear mandates and accountability.

- Integrate water management across agriculture, energy, cities, and industry.

- Implement transboundary water cooperation agreements between countries sharing rivers and aquifers.

Operational Timeline: All major shared basins have cooperation frameworks by 2027.

3. Expand Access to Water and Sanitation Technologies

- Deploy low-cost, scalable technologies (e.g., solar water purification, mobile sanitation units, community filtration systems).

- Invest in innovation hubs for water and sanitation startups, especially in developing countries.

Operational Timeline: Affordable technology solutions available to 80% of low-income communities by 2027.

4. Strengthen Community Ownership and Capacity Building

- Train local water committees and community-led sanitation groups.

- Build awareness campaigns on water conservation, hygiene practices, and system maintenance.

Operational Timeline: Local water governance systems active in all rural and peri-urban areas by 2026.

5. Monitor Progress with Smart Data and Real-Time Systems

- Establish real-time water quality and access monitoring systems using satellite data, IoT sensors, and mobile platforms.
- Publish open-access dashboards tracking SDG 6 indicators Nationally and Globally.

Operational Timeline: Global SDG 6 Water and Sanitation Monitoring Platform live by 2026.

In Summary: Fast-Track Priorities for SDG 6 (Clean Water and Sanitation)

Priority Area	Goal by 2030
Universal water and sanitation access	Safely managed services for all
Water quality and pollution reduction	50% reduction in untreated wastewater
Integrated water management	IWRM plans implemented Globally
Climate-resilient infrastructure	New infrastructure climate-proofed
Ecosystem protection and restoration	Water-related ecosystems rehabilitated
Smart monitoring and data	Real-time water systems operational

Visual Roadmap: Reaching SDG 6 (Clean Water and Sanitation) Targets by 2030

[Timeline Layout: Horizontal, milestones for each year 2025–2030]

2025: Foundation Year – Acceleration of Access and Governance Reform

- Launch National acceleration plans for universal water and sanitation coverage.

- Establish or strengthen National water authorities for integrated water governance.

- Mobilize blended finance models for water and sanitation investment.

2026: Infrastructure Expansion and Smart Monitoring Systems

- Deploy affordable, scalable water and sanitation technologies to rural, urban, and displaced communities.

- Operationalize National real-time water monitoring systems (IoT, AI, mobile).

- Expand community-led water governance models at the local level.

2027: Water Quality, Climate Resilience, and Ecosystem Restoration

- Halve untreated wastewater Globally through new treatment plants and nature-based solutions.

- Climate-proof new water and sanitation infrastructure against floods, droughts, and storms.

- Rehabilitate critical rivers, lakes, wetlands, and watersheds.

2028: Efficiency, Innovation, and Cross-Border Cooperation

- Strengthen cross-sector water coordination across

agriculture, energy, and cities.

- Accelerate innovation hubs for water-saving technologies and sanitation startups.

- Expand transboundary water cooperation agreements for shared rivers and aquifers.

2029: Final System Integration and Global Scaling

- Scale successful community water management models Globally.

- Finalize universal basic access coverage for water, sanitation, and hygiene services (WASH).

- Share Global best practices through UN platforms and regional summits.

2030: Achievement of SDG 6 Goals

- Universal access to safe drinking water, sanitation, and hygiene services.

- Climate-resilient and equitable water systems operational Globally.

- Significant improvement in water quality and restoration of ecosystems worldwide. You said:

- Adoption by Business Leaders: Will corporate leaders embrace sustainability as core to strategy or view it as a cost center?

- Global Standards for Sustainability: Will there be widespread adoption of measurable sustainability goals (e.g., circular economies)?

- Economic Constraints: How might Global economic challenges affect investment in Sustainable business Education?

- Collaboration Across Sectors: Will Education systems, governments, and businesses work together, or remain siloed?

Strategies and Operational Mechanisms to Achieve SDG 7: Affordable and Clean Energy by 2030

A. Strategies (What Needs to Be Done)

1. Ensure Universal Access to Affordable, Reliable, and Modern Energy Services

- Prioritize rural electrification programs, especially in Sub-Saharan Africa and South Asia.

- Deploy off-grid renewable energy solutions (solar home systems, mini-grids, micro-hydro).

- Subsidize connection costs and lower tariffs for low-income households.

Goal: By 2027, 95% of Global population connected to electricity (grid or off-grid).

2. Substantially Increase the Share of Renewable Energy

- Scale investments in solar, wind, hydro, geothermal, and modern bioenergy.

- Accelerate the retirement of coal plants and transition from fossil fuels.

- Integrate renewable energy into National energy grids with storage solutions (batteries, pumped hydro).

Goal: By 2028, renewables supply at least 60% of new power generation capacity Globally.

3. Double the Rate of Improvement in Energy Efficiency

- Implement building codes, appliance standards, and industrial energy-saving programs.

- Promote energy-efficient cooling, heating, and lighting systems.

- Retrofit existing infrastructure (buildings, industries) with smart energy management systems.

Goal: By 2027, double the energy efficiency improvement rate (based on 2010 baseline).

4. Expand Clean Cooking Solutions

- Deploy clean cookstoves, LPG, biogas, electric cooking, and solar cooking technologies.

- Integrate clean cooking access into National energy, climate, and health strategies.

Goal: By 2027, reduce population relying on traditional biomass by 50%.

5. Strengthen Energy Systems Resilience and Climate Adaptation

- Build climate-resilient energy infrastructure (grids, off-grid systems, pipelines).

- Develop early warning systems for energy sector climate risks (storms, droughts, floods).

Goal: By 2028, climate resilience built into 90% of new energy infrastructure projects.

B. Operational Mechanisms (How to Deliver the Strategies)

1. Scale Up Financing for Clean Energy

- Increase clean energy investment to $4–5 trillion annually (tripling current Global levels).

- Mobilize blended finance: public funds, private capital, multilateral development banks (MDBs), and climate funds (like the Green Climate Fund).

- De-risk clean energy investments in emerging markets through guarantees and concessional finance.

Operational Timeline: Clean energy investment tripled Globally by 2026.

2. Reform Energy Policies and Regulations

- Eliminate fossil fuel subsidies and shift to incentives for renewable energy and energy efficiency.

- Mandate net-zero energy targets for key sectors (power, transport, buildings) through legislation.

- Streamline grid interconnection and licensing procedures to fast-track renewable projects.

Operational Timeline: Energy transition-friendly policies operational in all countries by 2026.

3. Strengthen Public-Private Partnerships (PPPs) for Energy Access

- Engage private companies in rural electrification, mini-grid development, and smart city energy solutions.

- Launch energy access challenge funds to incentivize innovation in off-grid markets.

Operational Timeline: Major PPP programs for energy access operational by 2026.

4. Build Human Capacity for the Clean Energy Transition

- Train millions of technicians, engineers, project managers, and entrepreneurs in clean energy technologies.

- Focus on women's participation in the energy workforce (especially in off-grid and clean cooking sectors).

- Strengthen partnerships between universities, technical institutes, and energy companies.

Operational Timeline: 5 million new clean energy jobs created by 2027 Globally.

5. Monitor Progress with Smart Energy Data Platforms

- Develop real-time energy access and efficiency tracking systems using satellite imagery, smart meters, and AI.

- Publish open data dashboards tracking progress on electrification, renewables, energy efficiency, and clean cooking.

Operational Timeline: Global SDG 7 energy tracking platform upgraded and widely used by 2026.

In Summary: Fast-Track Priorities for SDG 7 (Clean Energy)

Priority Area	Goal by 2030
Universal energy access	100% electrification, universal clean cooking access
Renewable energy share	60%+ of new power capacity from renewables
Energy efficiency	Double efficiency improvement rate
Climate resilience of energy systems	90% climate-proofed new infrastructure
Sustainable energy financing	$4–5 trillion annual clean energy investment
Smart monitoring and open data	Real-time Global SDG 7 progress tracking

Tone for 2025–2030:

Ambitious, Fast-Tracking, Just, Climate-Resilient, Innovation-Led, People-Centered.

Visual Roadmap: Reaching SDG 7 (Affordable and Clean Energy) Targets by 2030

[Timeline Layout: Horizontal format — milestones from 2025 to 2030]

2025: Foundation Year – Energy Access Expansion and Policy Reform

- Launch National energy access acceleration programs (grid expansion + off-grid solutions).

- Reform National energy policies: eliminate fossil fuel

subsidies and introduce incentives for renewables and energy efficiency.

- Kickstart clean energy financing platforms (de-risking for private investors).

2026: Renewable Energy Scale-Up and Financing Surge

- Massively scale solar, wind, hydro, geothermal projects, especially in emerging economies.

- Triple clean energy investment Globally (blended public-private models).

- Deploy mini-grids and solar home systems in rural and remote regions.

2027: Energy Efficiency, Clean Cooking, and Skills Development

- Implement large-scale energy efficiency programs across industries, buildings, and transportation.

- Expand National clean cooking programs to halve traditional biomass use.

- Train millions of clean energy workers, with a focus on women and youth.

2028: Climate Resilience and Smart Energy Systems Expansion

- Integrate energy-climate adaptation measures into all new projects (flood, drought, heat resilience).

- Modernize power grids with smart technologies (smart meters, AI-based energy management).

- Advance cross-sector integration (energy-water-agriculture linkages).

2029: Global Best Practice Consolidation and Final Access Push

- Scale up best practice models for decentralized renewable energy and energy access solutions.

- Finalize near-universal electrification and access to affordable, clean energy services Globally.

- Strengthen International cooperation for Global energy transition.

2030: Achievement of SDG 7 Goals

- 100% access to affordable, reliable, Sustainable, and modern energy services worldwide.

- Majority renewable energy share in Global energy mix.

- Strong, climate-resilient, efficient energy systems established Globally.

Strategies and Operational Mechanisms to Achieve SDG 8: Decent Work and Economic Growth by 2030

A. Strategies (What Needs to Be Done)

1. Create Decent and Productive Employment for All

- Stimulate labor-intensive industries (manufacturing, green infrastructure, health, Education, rural development).

- Expand youth employment programs (internships, apprenticeships, entrepreneurship support).

- Prioritize women's economic empowerment and gender parity in labor force participation.

Goal: By 2027, substantial reduction in youth unemployment, gender employment gaps, and informal sector reliance.

2. Support Inclusive, Resilient, and Sustainable Economic Growth

- Foster micro, small, and medium-sized enterprises (MSMEs) with easier access to finance, digital markets, and training.

- Transition to green and digital economies with support for innovation hubs and start-ups.

- Strengthen rural economies (agriculture, agro-processing, eco-tourism, Sustainable infrastructure).

Goal: By 2026, inclusive GDP growth that is employment-rich and climate-resilient.

3. Promote Labor Rights, Safe Workplaces, and Social Protection

- Enforce labor rights standards (ILO conventions) on wages, working conditions, collective bargaining, and occupational safety.

- Expand universal social protection systems (pensions, unemployment benefits, maternity leave, health insurance).

- Combat forced labor, modern slavery, human trafficking, and child labor.

Goal: By 2027, achieve substantial progress in safe working environments and basic social protection coverage.

4. Boost Productivity and Economic Diversification

- Enhance access to technology, R&D investment, and innovation ecosystems for businesses.

- Facilitate value chain upgrades and industrial diversification in low- and middle-income economies.

- Invest in Education-to-work pathways emphasizing future skills (digital literacy, green skills, entrepreneurial thinking).

Goal: By 2028, substantial productivity increases across sectors, particularly for MSMEs and rural industries.

5. Strengthen Global Economic Governance and Fair Trade

- Support Global financial reform to enable more investment in Sustainable growth.

- Strengthen multilateral trade systems that promote fair, inclusive, and Sustainable trade practices.

- Encourage ethical supply chains and corporate responsibility (aligned with ESG principles).

Goal: By 2028, fair Global trade systems and corporate practices aligned with SDG 8 principles.

B. Operational Mechanisms (How to Deliver the Strategies)

1. Mobilize Massive Public and Private Investment in Decent Work

- Direct National recovery plans and development

financing toward job creation, especially in green sectors, SMEs, and public services.

- Mobilize impact investing and SDG-aligned finance to create Sustainable jobs and businesses.

Operational Timeline: By 2026, National and International investment strategies prioritize decent work and inclusive growth.

2. Accelerate Digital and Green Transitions

- Promote digital upskilling and reskilling programs for workers in all sectors.

- Invest in green economy programs (renewables, energy efficiency, Sustainable transport, climate-smart agriculture).

- Create future-ready labor markets that embrace automation and technological change ethically.

Operational Timeline: By 2027, green and digital sectors become major job creators worldwide.

3. Expand Social Protection Floors

- Scale universal social protection systems funded through progressive taxation and innovative finance (e.g., solidarity taxes, carbon pricing revenues).

- Formalize informal sector workers into social protection systems through tailored policies.

Operational Timeline: By 2026, basic social protection floors in place in all countries.

4. Strengthen Policy Coherence and Multi-Stakeholder Partnerships

- Coordinate across ministries of labor, finance, Education, and trade to drive inclusive economic growth agendas.

- Engage employers, workers' organizations, NGOs, and private sector alliances to co-create decent work strategies.

Operational Timeline: By 2025, National tripartite labor and economic councils functional in all countries.

5. Improve Labor Market Data, Monitoring, and Accountability

- Strengthen labor statistics systems for real-time tracking of employment, informality, social protection, wages, and workplace safety.

- Develop National SDG 8 dashboards for annual public reporting and policy adjustment.

Operational Timeline: By 2026, real-time SDG 8 monitoring systems operational Globally.

In Summary: Fast-Track Priorities for SDG 8 (Decent Work and Economic Growth)

Priority Area	Goal by 2030
Universal access to decent work	Significant drop in unemployment, informality
Inclusive economic growth	GDP growth inclusive and Sustainable
Strong social protection systems	Universal coverage achieved

Green and digital job creation	Major employment drivers
Labor rights and workplace safety	Fully enforced Globally
Smart monitoring and accountability	Real-time SDG 8 tracking

Tone for 2025–2030:

Inclusive, Sustainable, Innovation-Driven, Rights-Based, Growth-Oriented, Just Transition-Focused.

Visual Roadmap: Reaching SDG 8 (Decent Work and Economic Growth) Targets by 2030

[Timeline Layout: Horizontal format — milestones from 2025 to 2030]

2025: Foundation Year – Investment, Policy, and Partnership Acceleration

- Launch National decent work acceleration plans.

- Scale up public and private investment in job creation sectors (green economy, SMEs, digital economy).

- Strengthen social dialogue platforms between government, employers, and workers' organizations.

2026: Universal Social Protection Systems Expansion

- Implement universal basic social protection floors (pensions, health insurance, unemployment protection).

- Formalize informal sector workers into labor and social protection systems.

- Ensure basic workplace rights (minimum wages, safe

working conditions) are legally enforced.

2027: Digital and Green Jobs Transformation

- Launch National green jobs programs in energy, transport, Sustainable agriculture, construction.

- Scale digital upskilling and reskilling programs for youth and displaced workers.

- Expand access to finance and innovation hubs for MSMEs and entrepreneurs.

2028: Inclusive Growth, Productivity, and Trade Systems Strengthening

- Boost productivity through investment in technology, research, and value chain development.

- Enhance inclusive trade opportunities for low-income countries and small businesses.

- Advance ethical Global supply chains aligned with labor rights and sustainability.

2029: Global Best Practice Consolidation and Labor Governance Strengthening

- Scale up Global sharing of successful labor rights models and decent work initiatives.

- Strengthen labor market resilience against automation, Climate Change, and future economic shocks.

- Finalize National and Global monitoring dashboards for SDG 8 progress.

2030: Achievement of SDG 8 Goals

- Universal access to decent jobs, social protection, and safe workplaces.

- Sustainable, inclusive, and resilient economic growth realized Globally.

- Equal opportunities for all genders, ages, and communities in the world of work.

Strategies and Operational Mechanisms to Achieve SDG 9: Industry, Innovation, and Infrastructure by 2030

A. Strategies (What Needs to Be Done)

1. Build Quality, Sustainable, and Resilient Infrastructure

- Prioritize green, climate-resilient infrastructure — roads, energy, transport, water, ICT (information and communications technology).

- Expand rural and urban infrastructure (roads, bridges, renewable energy grids, fiber optic connectivity).

- Promote nature-based infrastructure solutions where appropriate (e.g., green roofs, natural flood defenses).

Goal: By 2027, all new National infrastructure projects are climate-resilient and inclusive.

2. Promote Sustainable Industrialization and Economic Diversification

- Modernize industries through cleaner technologies, resource-efficient processes, and low-carbon manufacturing.

- Strengthen domestic MSMEs (Micro, Small, and Medium-sized Enterprises) and local supply chains.

- Encourage value-added production (e.g., agro-processing, Sustainable textiles, electric vehicle assembly).

Goal: By 2028, substantial increase in industry's share of employment and GDP, especially in developing countries.

3. Foster Innovation Ecosystems and Technology Development

- Increase investment in R&D, especially in clean energy, AI, biotech, and Sustainable manufacturing.

- Establish National innovation hubs, tech parks, and startup incubators.

- Promote universal access to affordable, reliable Internet and bridge the digital divide.

Goal: By 2027, significant increase in R&D spending as a share of GDP Globally.

4. Enhance Regional and Cross-Border Infrastructure Connectivity

- Develop regional infrastructure corridors (roads, energy grids, digital infrastructure) to link economies.

- Strengthen trade facilitation and transboundary transportation systems (railways, ports, airports).

- Support regional industrial value chains for inclusive growth.

Goal: By 2028, major regional connectivity programs completed across Africa, Asia, and Latin America.

5. Transition to Smart, Circular, and Low-Carbon Industries

- Promote circular economy models (recycling, re-manufacturing, Sustainable product design).

- Encourage green industrial policies (incentives for clean energy use, carbon-neutral factories).

- Deploy Industry 4.0 technologies (automation, IoT, AI) responsibly to maximize sustainability.

Goal: By 2028, significant portion of industrial output from Sustainable and circular models.

B. Operational Mechanisms (How to Deliver the Strategies)

1. Mobilize Massive Public-Private Investments in Infrastructure and Innovation

- Increase infrastructure investment to at least 5–6% of GDP annually.

- Mobilize blended finance (public, private, multilateral development banks, climate finance).

- Establish Innovation Impact Funds for tech development and startup ecosystems.

Operational Timeline: Major National infrastructure and innovation funds operational by 2026.

2. Update and Align Policies, Regulations, and Standards

- Modernize industrial and infrastructure policies to prioritize green, resilient, inclusive growth.

- Standardize smart infrastructure regulations (e.g., green

building codes, smart city guidelines, clean energy targets).

Operational Timeline: Green and resilient infrastructure standards mandatory in all countries by 2026.

3. Expand Digital Connectivity and Technology Access

- Deploy fiber optic networks, 5G infrastructure, and broadband for all in rural and urban areas.

- Subsidize digital access for marginalized groups, schools, and MSMEs.

Operational Timeline: Universal affordable Internet access Globally by 2027.

4. Support Industrial Upgrading and MSME Empowerment

- Provide technical assistance, financing, and digital transformation support to small and medium enterprises.

- Link MSMEs to Sustainable industrial value chains through innovation platforms and partnerships.

Operational Timeline: MSMEs contributing significantly to industrial output by 2027.

5. Strengthen Monitoring, Reporting, and Innovation Metrics

- Build National SDG 9 monitoring dashboards covering infrastructure resilience, industrial modernization, digital access, and innovation outputs.

- Create open innovation data portals for entrepreneurs, investors, and policymakers.

Operational Timeline: Real-time infrastructure and industry

innovation tracking operational Globally by 2026.

In Summary: Fast-Track Priorities for SDG 9 (Industry, Innovation, Infrastructure)

Priority Area	Goal by 2030
Sustainable, resilient infrastructure	100% new projects climate-resilient
Sustainable industrialization	Increase industry's share in GDP and employment
R&D investment and innovation expansion	Major innovation hubs operational
Universal digital connectivity	100% affordable Internet access
Circular economy and green industries	Significant portion of industry Sustainable

Tone for 2025–2030:

Green, Digital, Inclusive, Resilient, Innovation-Driven, Future-Ready.

Visual Roadmap: Reaching SDG 9 (Industry, Innovation, and Infrastructure) Targets by 2030

[Timeline Layout: Horizontal format — milestones for each year from 2025 to 2030]

2025: Foundation Year – Infrastructure Expansion and Policy Modernization

- Launch National infrastructure modernization plans prioritizing green, inclusive, and resilient projects.

- Modernize industrial policies to incentivize Sustainable

production and innovation ecosystems.

- Kickstart blended finance initiatives for infrastructure and R&D investments.

2026: Smart Infrastructure and Digital Connectivity Acceleration

- Deploy nationwide broadband networks and 5G infrastructure, including rural regions.

- Enforce green infrastructure standards (green building codes, smart city regulations).

- Expand access to affordable Internet services for underserved populations.

2027: Industrial Upgrading, MSME Support, and Innovation Hubs

- Launch National programs to modernize industries with clean technologies and resource-efficient processes.

- Create innovation hubs, incubators, and startup support platforms in all major regions.

- Integrate MSMEs into Sustainable and resilient value chains.

2028: Circular Economy Scaling and Cross-Border Connectivity

- Promote circular economy models across industrial sectors.

- Expand regional infrastructure corridors (transport, digital, energy) for cross-border economic growth.

- Advance smart manufacturing (Industry 4.0) responsibly.

2029: Global Best Practice Consolidation and Innovation Leadership

- Scale up Global cooperation on green and digital industrialization.

- Expand research and development partnerships for clean technology, AI, biotech, and energy innovation.

- Finalize National SDG 9 achievement reviews and innovation benchmarking.

2030: Achievement of SDG 9 Goals

- Universal access to resilient infrastructure and affordable digital connectivity.

- Sustainable industrialization mainstreamed Globally.

- Dynamic innovation ecosystems driving inclusive and green economic growth.

Strategies and Operational Mechanisms to Achieve SDG 10: Reduced Inequalities by 2030

now we move to SDG 10: Reduced Inequalities, which is critical because without closing the gaps — between income groups, genders, ethnicities, regions, and nations — no other SDG can be truly achieved.

Since we are now in the final five years toward 2030, bold, systemic, equity-driven strategies are necessary. Here's the full action plan — strategies and operational mechanisms — to achieve SDG 10:

A. Strategies (What Needs to Be Done)

1. Reduce Income Inequality Within Countries

- Implement progressive taxation systems (higher taxes on wealth, inheritance, luxury goods).

- Expand living wages, social transfers, and safety nets for low-income groups.

- Boost employment opportunities in marginalized and rural areas.

Goal: By 2026, significantly reduce the income share gap between the richest 10% and poorest 40%.

2. Eliminate Discrimination and Promote Social Inclusion

- Pass and enforce anti-discrimination laws (race, ethnicity, gender, disability, age, migration status).

- Create inclusive Education, healthcare, and employment programs targeted at marginalized groups.

- Ensure equal access to justice, political participation, and public services.

Goal: By 2027, legal protection against discrimination in all countries.

3. Empower Migrants, Refugees, and Displaced Persons

- Ensure safe, orderly, and responsible migration pathways.

- Grant equal rights to migrants in labor markets, Education, and health systems.

- Protect refugee and displaced populations under National development plans.

Goal: By 2027, full integration of migrants and refugees into National systems in most countries.

4. Strengthen Economic Inclusion through Fair Trade and Global Governance

- Reform Global trade systems to be more equitable for developing countries.

- Ensure debt relief and financial support for low-income nations to build resilience.

- Promote inclusive digital economies by connecting marginalized communities.

Goal: By 2028, increase share of Global trade and financial flows benefiting developing countries.

5. Close Gaps in Access to Digital Technology and Financial Services

- Expand Internet access, mobile services, and affordable digital tools to underserved areas.

- Promote financial inclusion through mobile banking, microfinance, and inclusive fintech solutions.

Goal: By 2027, at least 90% of populations connected digitally and financially.

B. Operational Mechanisms (How to Deliver the Strategies)

1. Scale Up Social Protection Systems for All

- Build universal social protection floors: pensions, unemployment insurance, child benefits, disability support.

- Target marginalized and vulnerable groups specifically (ethnic minorities, women, disabled persons).

Operational Timeline: Social protection systems expanded in all countries by 2026.

2. Implement Equity-Focused National Development Plans

- Require all National development plans to include equity impact assessments.

- Mandate inclusive budgeting processes to ensure marginalized voices shape policy priorities.

Operational Timeline: Equity-focused National plans adopted Globally by 2026.

3. Mobilize Financial Resources for Inclusion

- Mobilize International finance, remittances facilitation, and innovative solidarity taxes (e.g., financial transaction taxes, carbon taxes) to fund inequality-reduction programs.

- Support South-South and Triangular Cooperation for local solutions.

Operational Timeline: New financing models supporting inclusion operational by 2027.

4. Enhance Data Collection and Disaggregated Monitoring

- Build National data systems disaggregated by income, gender, ethnicity, disability, age, location.

- Publish annual Inequality Dashboards tracking progress on income gaps, Education gaps, health gaps, and digital gaps.

Operational Timeline: Disaggregated inequality monitoring operational Globally by 2026.

5. Empower Grassroots Movements and Social Dialogue

- Invest in civil society organizations, community groups, and local leaders working on inclusion and anti-discrimination.

- Strengthen social dialogue mechanisms to ensure marginalized groups have a voice in National decision-making.

Operational Timeline: Community-driven inequality reduction programs expanded by 2027.

In Summary: Fast-Track Priorities for SDG 10 (Reduced Inequalities)

Priority Area	Goal by 2030
Income equality	Major reduction in top vs. bottom income gaps
Anti-discrimination and social inclusion	Equal rights protection in all countries
Migration and refugee rights	Full integration into social and economic systems
Financial and digital inclusion	90% of populations digitally and financially included
Fair trade and debt reform	More equitable Global systems
Smart monitoring and data	Disaggregated progress tracking operational

Tone for 2025–2030:

Equity-Centered, Justice-Oriented, Systemic, Inclusive Growth-Driven, People-Led.

Visual Roadmap: Reaching SDG 10 (Reduced Inequalities) Targets by 2030

[Timeline Layout: Horizontal, clean format — milestones for each year 2025–2030]

2025: Foundation Year – Policy Reforms and Equity Planning

- Launch National inequality reduction strategies focused on income, gender, ethnic, and regional gaps.

- Strengthen progressive tax systems and social protection expansion targeting the bottom 40%.

- Pass and enforce anti-discrimination laws Nationally.

2026: Universal Social Protection and Digital Inclusion Scaling

- Establish or expand universal social protection systems for all citizens.

- Roll out affordable Internet access programs for rural, low-income, and marginalized communities.

- Implement National inclusive budgeting and equity-based development planning.

2027: Migrant and Refugee Rights, Financial Inclusion Boost

- Integrate migrants, refugees, and displaced populations

into National services and economies.

- Scale up mobile banking, microfinance, and digital payment systems for underserved communities.

- Expand targeted Education and skills training programs for marginalized youth.

2028: Fair Trade, Global Financial System Reform, and Cross-Border Inclusion

- Support Global reforms for fairer trade terms and financial flows benefiting developing economies.

- Advance debt relief programs to empower least developed countries (LDCs) toward Sustainable growth.

- Expand cross-border programs for migrant protection and remittances facilitation.

2029: Consolidation of Inclusion Best Practices and Final Acceleration Push

- Scale up best practices in inclusive social and economic programs.

- Finalize annual inequality reduction reviews linked to SDG 10 indicators.

- Promote community-driven action plans in all regions to bridge last-mile gaps.

2030: Achievement of SDG 10 Goals

- Reduced income and opportunity inequalities across all countries.

- Universal access to rights, services, and decent livelihoods.

- Global systems reformed toward fairness, resilience, and shared prosperity.

now onto SDG 11: Sustainable Cities and Communities — a hugely important SDG because by 2030, nearly 60% of the world's population will live in cities. Urban areas must be safe, inclusive, resilient, Sustainable, and climate-smart to achieve the full SDG agenda.

Since we have only five years left, achieving SDG 11 requires aggressive, multi-Sectoral urban action. Here's your full strategic and operational guide:

Strategies and Operational Mechanisms to Achieve SDG 11: Sustainable Cities and Communities by 2030

A. Strategies (What Needs to Be Done)

1. Accelerate the Development of Affordable and Inclusive Housing

- Massively scale affordable, safe, climate-resilient housing programs for low-income populations.

- Upgrade and regularize slums, informal settlements, and peri-urban areas.

- Implement pro-poor housing policies ensuring access to land, infrastructure, and basic services.

Goal: By 2027, substantially reduce the number of people living in slums and inadequate housing.

2. Build Safe, Inclusive, and Sustainable Public Spaces and Infrastructure

- Expand and protect parks, public squares, sidewalks,

cycling lanes, and accessible urban spaces.

- Design cities for people-first mobility (pedestrians, bikes, public transport) — not just cars.

- Prioritize safety, accessibility, and inclusion for women, children, the elderly, and persons with disabilities.

Goal: By 2026, ensure universal access to safe, inclusive public spaces in all major cities.

3. Strengthen Urban Climate Resilience and Disaster Risk Reduction

- Implement urban climate adaptation plans (green roofs, flood barriers, tree canopies, heat action plans).

- Build resilient infrastructure able to withstand floods, droughts, storms, and rising sea levels.

- Ensure early warning systems and disaster recovery strategies are operational citywide.

Goal: By 2027, 100% of cities have operational climate-resilient urban plans.

4. Expand Sustainable Urban Transport Systems

- Invest in affordable, accessible, clean public transportation systems (buses, metros, light rail, e-bikes).

- Electrify public and private vehicle fleets through incentives.

- Promote transit-oriented development (compact, walkable cities around transport hubs).

Goal: By 2028, major cities achieve low-carbon public transport access for all.

5. Integrate Smart City Technologies for Sustainability and Efficiency

- Deploy smart city platforms (IoT, AI, data dashboards) for urban energy, water, waste, mobility, and public safety.

- Use open data platforms to enhance citizen participation and transparent governance.

- Foster urban innovation hubs to pilot smart, green technologies at the local level.

Goal: By 2028, smart city initiatives operational in all major cities Globally.

B. Operational Mechanisms (How to Deliver the Strategies)

1. Mobilize Urban Finance and Investment in Sustainability

- Create Urban Green Investment Funds pooling public budgets, private finance, and climate finance.

- Develop municipal bonds and SDG-aligned urban finance mechanisms to fund Sustainable housing, transport, energy, and public services.

Operational Timeline: Urban green finance platforms scaled Globally by 2026.

2. Strengthen City Governance and Urban Policy Frameworks

- Empower local and municipal governments with financing authority, planning capacity, and legal frameworks aligned to SDG 11.

- Promote participatory urban planning involving all community groups, especially marginalized communities.

Operational Timeline: SDG 11-aligned urban governance frameworks adopted by 2026.

3. Expand Resilient and Inclusive Basic Services

- Invest in urban water, sanitation, solid waste management, and energy systems to ensure safe and Sustainable access for all.

- Prioritize service delivery in underserved communities, including informal settlements.

Operational Timeline: Universal urban access to basic services significantly expanded by 2027.

4. Strengthen Urban Data Systems and Monitoring

- Build real-time urban dashboards tracking air quality, housing affordability, public safety, disaster risks, and inclusivity indicators.

- Integrate geospatial and satellite data into urban planning and management.

Operational Timeline: Smart urban data platforms operational in major cities by 2027.

5. Foster Regional and Global Urban Partnerships

- Participate actively in Global city networks like C40, ICLEI, UCLG, UN-Habitat platforms.

- Strengthen South-South cooperation for urban innovation and resilience sharing.

Operational Timeline: Global city partnerships for SDG 11 scaled up by 2026.

In Summary: Fast-Track Priorities for SDG 11 (Sustainable Cities and Communities)

Priority Area	Goal by 2030
Affordable and resilient housing	Slum upgrading and inclusive housing access
Safe, inclusive public spaces	Universal access to parks, sidewalks, safe streets
Urban climate resilience	Climate-ready urban infrastructure everywhere
Sustainable transport systems	Low-carbon, affordable public transport access
Smart cities and digital innovation	Major cities running smart, green systems
Urban governance and finance strengthening	Empowered cities driving SDG 11 innovation

Tone for 2025–2030:

People-Centered, Climate-Resilient, Inclusive, Tech-Enabled, Finance-Backed, Transformative Urbanization.

Visual Roadmap: Reaching SDG 11 (Sustainable Cities and Communities) Targets by 2030

[Timeline Layout: Horizontal format — milestones for each year 2025–2030]

2025: Foundation Year – Urban Policy Reform and Financing Mobilization

- Launch National and city-level SDG 11 action plans

focused on inclusive, resilient urban growth.

- Establish Urban Green Investment Funds and issue municipal SDG bonds.

- Strengthen local governance structures to align city planning with sustainability and inclusivity.

2026: Affordable Housing and Basic Services Expansion

- Accelerate affordable housing programs for low-income, marginalized, and displaced populations.

- Expand basic urban services: water, sanitation, energy, waste management.

- Formalize and upgrade slums and informal settlements sustainably.

2027: Urban Climate Resilience and Public Space Transformation

- Implement urban climate adaptation projects (green infrastructure, flood defenses, heat action plans).

- Expand safe, inclusive public spaces (parks, cycle lanes, accessible sidewalks).

- Establish early warning systems for urban disaster risks.

2028: Sustainable Transport Systems and Smart City Innovation

- Build and electrify mass public transit systems (metros, buses, light rail, e-bikes).

- Deploy smart city solutions for traffic, waste, energy, and citizen engagement.

- Achieve affordable, low-carbon mobility access for all city residents.

2029: Global Urban Innovation Scaling and Final Urban Inclusion Push

- Scale best practices from Sustainable, inclusive cities worldwide.

- Finalize inclusive, resilient urban development goals across all cities.

- Share innovations Globally via C40, ICLEI, UN-Habitat networks.

2030: Achievement of SDG 11 Goals

- All urban residents access safe housing, transport, and public spaces.

- Cities are climate-resilient, inclusive, digitally smart, and sustainably growing.

- Urban ecosystems support prosperity, equity, and environmental stewardship for all.

Strategies and Operational Mechanisms to Achieve SDG 12: Responsible Consumption and Production by 2030

now focusing on SDG 12: Responsible Consumption and Production, one of the most transformational goals because it touches industries, cities, agriculture, households, and Global supply chains. Without fixing how we produce, consume, and waste, achieving the 2030 Agenda is impossible.

Since only five years remain, the work for SDG 12 must be accelerated, systemic, and circular economy-driven. Here's the full strategies and operational mechanisms guide:

A. Strategies (What Needs to Be Done)

1. Accelerate the Transition to Circular Economy Models

- Promote waste prevention, reuse, recycling, and closed-loop production across all industries.

- Incentivize eco-design: products that are durable, repairable, recyclable.

- Support urban mining, remanufacturing, and secondary materials markets.

Goal: By 2027, significant portion of Global industries adopt circular economy practices.

2. Scale Sustainable Business Practices Across Industries

- Require companies to implement Sustainable production standards and responsible supply chains.

- Strengthen Environmental, Social, Governance (ESG) disclosure and corporate accountability laws.

- Support SMEs in greening their operations (energy efficiency, cleaner production, resource optimization).

Goal: By 2026, sustainability reporting mandatory for large businesses Globally.

3. Empower Sustainable Consumer Choices

- Expand eco-labeling, product transparency, and sustainability certifications.

- Promote Sustainable lifestyles campaigns — focusing on food waste, energy use, fashion, plastics, and travel habits.

- Make Sustainable products affordable and accessible for all consumers.

Goal: By 2027, Sustainable consumer options widely available in all major markets.

4. Minimize Food Loss and Waste

- Strengthen farm-to-market value chains to prevent harvest and post-harvest losses.

- Promote consumer-level campaigns to reduce food waste.

- Support circular food systems (e.g., composting, food rescue programs).

Goal: By 2028, halve Global per capita food waste at retail and consumer levels.

5. Promote Green Public Procurement (GPP) and Sustainable Infrastructure

- Require governments to purchase eco-friendly goods and services.

- Align public infrastructure projects with Sustainable construction standards and low-carbon targets.

Goal: By 2027, green public procurement policies operational in 100% of National governments.

B. Operational Mechanisms (How to Deliver the Strategies)

1. Reform Subsidies and Incentives Toward Sustainability

- Phase out fossil fuel, chemical, and resource-depleting subsidies.

- Redirect subsidies toward renewables, Sustainable agriculture, eco-innovation, and circular economy initiatives.

Operational Timeline: Environmentally harmful subsidies phased out Globally by 2026.

2. Strengthen Regulatory Frameworks and International Agreements

- Pass and enforce laws on eco-design, waste reduction, plastics phase-out, and carbon footprint labeling.

- Enhance International cooperation on pollution control, resource conservation, and green trade rules.

Operational Timeline: Comprehensive SDG 12-aligned policies adopted Globally by 2027.

3. Expand Research, Innovation, and Technology Deployment

- Invest in clean technologies for production, waste management, circular business models.

- Support green innovation hubs and Sustainable entrepreneurship incubators.

Operational Timeline: Major R&D investment surges for circular economy solutions by 2026.

4. Raise Awareness and Build Consumer Demand for Sustainability

- Launch Global Education campaigns on Sustainable consumption and production.

- Integrate sustainability Education into school curricula, vocational training, and lifelong learning platforms.

Operational Timeline: Global Sustainable consumption awareness campaigns scaled by 2026.

5. Build Monitoring Systems for Sustainable Consumption and Production

- Develop National SCP dashboards tracking waste, materials efficiency, Sustainable procurement, corporate ESG reporting.

- Harmonize indicators Internationally to measure progress on consumption and production patterns.

Operational Timeline: Real-time SCP monitoring platforms operational Globally by 2027.

In Summary: Fast-Track Priorities for SDG 12 (Responsible Consumption and Production)

Priority Area	Goal by 2030
Circular economy adoption	Major industries shift to circular models
Sustainable business and supply chains	Sustainability reporting universal
Sustainable consumer choices	Eco-labeling and access widespread
Food loss and waste reduction	Per capita food waste cut by 50%
Green public procurement	GPP mainstreamed Globally
Monitoring and data	SCP progress tracking operational

Tone for 2025–2030:

Circular, Regenerative, Consumer-Led, Innovation-Driven,

Systems-Change-Focused

Visual Roadmap: Reaching SDG 12 (Responsible Consumption and Production) Targets by 2030

[Timeline Layout: Horizontal — milestones year-by-year from 2025 to 2030]

2025: Foundation Year – Circular Economy and Policy Reform Launch

- Adopt National circular economy strategies focusing on resource efficiency, waste prevention, and green design.

- Reform subsidies and incentives to eliminate support for polluting industries.

- Launch National SCP (Sustainable Consumption and Production) action plans.

2026: Corporate Accountability and Sustainable Production Scaling

- Mandate sustainability reporting and responsible supply chain practices for major companies.

- Support MSMEs in green transition through financing and technical assistance.

- Expand green innovation hubs and Sustainable entrepreneurship incubators.

2027: Sustainable Consumer Lifestyles and Food Waste Reduction

- Launch National and Global Sustainable lifestyles campaigns (eco-labels, consumer Education).

- Expand food loss and waste reduction programs from farm to fork.

- Scale affordable access to eco-friendly products and services.

2028: Green Public Procurement and Circular Business Models Scaling

- Institutionalize green procurement policies in all levels of government.

- Accelerate adoption of circular business models in manufacturing, construction, textiles, and packaging industries.

- Strengthen Global cooperation on green standards and trade agreements.

2029: Smart Monitoring, Global Best Practices Consolidation

- Operationalize National SCP dashboards tracking consumption, production, and waste trends.

- Publish Global circular economy success stories and model replication guidelines.

- Prepare final SDG 12 achievement reviews Globally.

2030: Achievement of SDG 12 Goals

- Major industries operate under circular economy models.

- Sustainable consumption habits mainstreamed among Global consumers.

- Significant reduction in resource use, pollution, and waste at all levels.

Strategies and Operational Mechanisms to Achieve SDG 13: Climate Action by 2030

Now we focus on SDG 13: Climate Action, one of the most urgent SDGs. Without accelerated climate action, many other SDGs (poverty, health, food security, water, cities) will not be achieved.

Since only five years remain, radical, coordinated, and system-wide climate strategies are necessary. Here's the full strategies and operational mechanisms guide for SDG 13:

A. Strategies (What Needs to Be Done)

1. Rapidly Accelerate Decarbonization Across All Sectors

- Transition energy systems to 100% renewable energy (solar, wind, hydro, geothermal).

- Decarbonize transport, buildings, and heavy industry through electrification, hydrogen, and energy efficiency.

- Implement carbon pricing, carbon taxes, and emission trading systems Globally.

Goal: By 2027, halve Global greenhouse gas emissions compared to 2010 levels.

2. Scale Up Climate Adaptation and Resilience Measures

- Implement National climate adaptation plans in agriculture, water, health, cities, and coastal systems.

- Invest in climate-resilient infrastructure, nature-based solutions (mangroves, wetlands restoration), and early warning systems.

- Strengthen insurance and risk financing mechanisms for vulnerable communities.

Goal: By 2027, all countries have operational National adaptation plans.

3. Mobilize Massive Climate Finance

- Deliver the promised $100 billion per year in climate finance to developing countries.

- Expand public-private partnerships for green finance, climate bonds, and blended finance models.

- Create National climate investment platforms to absorb and deploy funds efficiently.

Goal: By 2026, climate finance flows doubled from 2020 levels.

4. Strengthen Climate Education, Advocacy, and Capacity Building

- Integrate Climate Change Education into National curricula at all levels.

- Support youth climate leadership, indigenous knowledge systems, and community-led action.

- Raise awareness through National campaigns linking climate to daily life impacts.

Goal: By 2026, 100% of National Education systems integrate climate literacy.

5. Foster Global Cooperation and Stronger Governance Mechanisms

- Strengthen commitments under the Paris Agreement

(update and implement enhanced NDCs).

- Promote net-zero alliances across public, private, and civil society sectors.

- Expand regional climate alliances (e.g., African Climate Initiative, ASEAN Climate Partnerships).

Goal: By 2027, all countries have updated, ambitious climate commitments aligned with 1.5°C pathway.

B. Operational Mechanisms (How to Deliver the Strategies)

1. Enhance Nationally Determined Contributions (NDCs) and Net-Zero Targets

- Make net-zero pledges mandatory through National legislation.

- Integrate climate targets into National development plans and budgets.

Operational Timeline: Net-zero targets and new NDCs fully legislated in all countries by 2026.

2. Build Green Job Markets and Just Transition Programs

- Create millions of green jobs in renewable energy, Sustainable agriculture, clean transport, and circular economy sectors.

- Implement just transition plans to support workers and communities dependent on high-carbon industries.

Operational Timeline: National just transition frameworks operational in all countries by 2026.

3. Strengthen Climate Risk Management and Disaster Preparedness

- Scale up early warning systems for extreme weather events Globally.

- Embed climate risk disclosure into financial and infrastructure planning.

- Build resilient agriculture systems using climate-smart techniques.

Operational Timeline: Early warning coverage extended to all populations by 2027.

4. Catalyze Technological Innovation for Mitigation and Adaptation

- Invest in green R&D: battery storage, carbon capture, drought-resistant crops, AI for climate modeling.

- Support climate innovation accelerators and partnerships between governments, businesses, and research institutes.

Operational Timeline: Major green technology investment surges Globally by 2026.

5. Implement Monitoring, Reporting, and Transparency Systems

- Develop National and Global MRV systems (Monitoring, Reporting, Verification) for emissions, adaptation, and finance.

- Make open-access climate data platforms publicly available.

Operational Timeline: Real-time climate action monitoring systems operational Globally by 2027.

In Summary: Fast-Track Priorities for SDG 13 (Climate Action)

Visual Roadmap: Reaching SDG 13 (Climate Action) Targets by 2030

[Timeline Layout: Horizontal — milestones year-by-year from 2025 to 2030]

2025: Foundation Year – Enhanced NDCs and Climate Finance Mobilization

- Update and enhance Nationally Determined Contributions (NDCs) aligned with 1.5°C goals.

- Scale up climate finance commitments and operationalize National climate investment platforms.

- Legislate National net-zero emissions targets.

2026: Climate Education, Green Jobs, and Adaptation Plans Rollout

- Integrate climate literacy into all Education levels.

- Launch National just transition programs (reskilling workers from high-carbon sectors).

- Operationalize National climate adaptation strategies across all sectors (health, agriculture, infrastructure).

2027: Emissions Reduction, Resilience Building, and Early Warning Expansion

- Achieve major emission cuts across energy, transport, industry, and agriculture.

- Implement full coverage of early warning systems for extreme weather.

- Strengthen climate risk disclosure frameworks for public and private sectors.

2028: Innovation, Nature-Based Solutions, and Regional Cooperation Expansion

- Scale up investments in green technologies (battery storage, carbon capture, regenerative agriculture).

- Massively expand nature-based solutions (reforestation, coastal ecosystem restoration).

- Strengthen regional climate action partnerships (Africa, Asia-Pacific, Latin America).

2029: Consolidation of Global Net-Zero Alliances and Final Acceleration Push

- Finalize net-zero transition roadmaps across countries, cities, industries, and financial systems.

- Scale best practices Globally and ensure multilevel governance coherence (local-National-Global).

- Prepare final 2030 SDG 13 progress reviews and verification.

2030: Achievement of SDG 13 Goals

- Global emissions halved from 2010 levels.

- Universal National adaptation coverage achieved.

- Climate-resilient, low-carbon development mainstreamed worldwide.

- Global pathways on track to limiting warming to 1.5°C.

Strategies and Operational Mechanisms to Achieve SDG 14: Life Below Water by 2030

Now we turn to SDG 14: Life Below Water, focused on conserving and sustainably using the oceans, seas, and marine resources. Oceans regulate our climate, feed billions, support livelihoods, and hold vast biodiversity — but they're under unprecedented pressure.

With only five years left, achieving SDG 14 requires urgent, coordinated ocean governance, Sustainable blue economy development, and restoration of marine ecosystems.

Here's the comprehensive strategy:

A. Strategies (What Needs to Be Done)

1. End Overfishing and Promote Sustainable Fisheries

- Enforce science-based fisheries management plans, including quotas and seasonal bans.

- Support the transition to Sustainable small-scale fisheries through training, financing, and equipment.

- Eliminate harmful fishing subsidies that encourage overfishing or illegal practices.

Goal: By 2026, rebuild overfished stocks and eliminate IUU (illegal, unreported, and unregulated) fishing.

2. Protect and Restore Marine Ecosystems

- Expand marine protected areas (MPAs) to cover at least 30% of ocean area ("30x30" target).

- Launch large-scale coral reef and mangrove restoration programs.

- Prevent coastal erosion and biodiversity loss through nature-based solutions.

Goal: By 2027, all nations have a National marine biodiversity protection and restoration strategy.

3. Reduce Marine Pollution (Plastic, Nutrients, Chemicals)

- Ban or restrict single-use plastics and promote circular economy solutions.

- Improve wastewater and stormwater treatment systems, especially near coasts.

- Strengthen Global agreements on marine pollution control and monitoring.

Goal: By 2028, reduce marine plastic pollution by 50% and nutrient pollution hotspots by 30%.

4. Advance a Sustainable Blue Economy

- Promote Sustainable aquaculture, ocean-based renewable energy, eco-tourism, and marine biotechnology.

- Develop blue economy investment frameworks and National strategies.

- Support inclusive coastal livelihoods and equitable benefit-sharing.

Goal: By 2027, blue economy becomes a core pillar in National economic planning for all coastal states.

5. Address Ocean-Climate Interlinkages

- Protect ocean carbon sinks (mangroves, seagrass beds, salt marshes).

- Reduce ocean acidification through strong Global emissions reduction and monitoring systems.

- Build coastal resilience against sea-level rise, hurricanes, and saltwater intrusion.

Goal: By 2028, all coastal countries have integrated ocean-climate resilience plans.

B. Operational Mechanisms (How to Deliver the Strategies)

1. Implement and Enforce Strong Ocean Governance

- Ratify and implement UN Convention on the Law of the Sea (UNCLOS) and the High Seas Treaty (BBNJ).

- Establish marine spatial planning frameworks to balance conservation, fisheries, and economic use.

- Use satellite surveillance to monitor IUU fishing and marine activity.

Timeline: National ocean governance frameworks operational by 2026 in all coastal and island states.

2. Mobilize Ocean Finance and Incentives

- Launch Blue Bonds and other Sustainable ocean financing instruments.

- Channel public and private investment into marine conservation, clean ports, and Sustainable fisheries.

- Ensure that climate finance mechanisms include ocean-based adaptation and mitigation.

Timeline: Blue finance mechanisms active in at least 75 countries by 2027.

3. Strengthen Ocean Science, Data, and Monitoring

- Support the UN Decade of Ocean Science (2021–2030).
- Establish real-time marine data platforms (ocean temperature, pollution levels, biodiversity health).
- Build local capacity for community-based marine monitoring.

Timeline: Global marine monitoring system aligned with SDG 14 indicators operational by 2026.

4. Build Local Capacity and Engage Coastal Communities

- Strengthen Education, awareness, and participation of fishers, youth, and women in marine conservation.
- Fund community-based marine protected areas and local marine stewardship initiatives.
- Protect indigenous marine knowledge and rights.

Timeline: Coastal community engagement programs scaled Globally by 2027.

In Summary: Fast-Track Priorities for SDG 14 (Life Below Water)

Priority Area	Goal by 2030
Sustainable fisheries	End IUU fishing and rebuild fish stocks
Marine biodiversity conservation	30% ocean area under effective protection
Marine pollution control	50% reduction in plastic and nutrient waste
Blue economy development	Core sector in National strategies
Ocean-climate resilience	All coastal countries climate-ready
Governance, finance, and data	Full coverage of SDG 14 governance systems

Tone for 2025–2030:

Urgent, Regenerative, Equity-Focused, Ocean-Literate, Climate-Aligned.

Visual Roadmap: Reaching SDG 14 (Life Below Water) Targets by 2030

[Timeline Layout: Horizontal — milestones year-by-year from 2025 to 2030]

2025: Foundation Year – Ocean Governance and Sustainable Fisheries Reform

- Strengthen National and Global frameworks (UNCLOS, High Seas Treaty implementation).

- Adopt Sustainable fisheries management plans to rebuild overexploited stocks.

- Launch blue economy investment strategies for coastal nations.

2026: Marine Ecosystem Protection and Pollution Reduction Acceleration

- Expand marine protected areas (MPAs) toward the 30x30 target.

- Ban/restrict single-use plastics Nationally and regionally.

- Implement coastal restoration projects (mangroves, seagrass, coral reefs).

2027: Sustainable Blue Economy Scaling and Community Mobilization

- Operationalize blue economy initiatives (Sustainable aquaculture, eco-tourism, ocean renewables).

- Mobilize coastal communities, indigenous groups, and small-scale fishers in marine conservation programs.

- Expand satellite surveillance and enforcement of marine laws.

2028: Climate-Ocean Resilience Systems Expansion

- Integrate ocean-based climate solutions into National climate plans (NDCs).

- Scale nature-based coastal defences against sea-level rise, erosion, and storms.

- Launch Global early warning systems for ocean and coastal risks.

2029: Consolidation of Blue Finance and Best Practice Sharing

- Scale up Blue Bonds and ocean conservation funds Globally.

- Publish best practices for marine protected areas, Sustainable fisheries, and pollution reduction.

- Prepare final SDG 14 achievement reviews Globally.

2030: Achievement of SDG 14 Goals

- 30% of oceans under effective protection.

- Sustainable, climate-resilient fisheries and blue economies operational worldwide.

- Marine pollution drastically reduced and ecosystems on a path to full recovery.

Now we focus on SDG 15: Life on Land, which is about protecting, restoring, and sustainably managing forests, ecosystems, biodiversity, and land resources. It's directly tied to climate action, food security, water supply, and human survival.

With only five years left, the world must act decisively to halt ecosystem degradation, prevent species loss, and scale nature-based solutions.

Here's your comprehensive action plan:

Strategies and Operational Mechanisms to Achieve SDG 15: Life on Land by 2030

A. Strategies (What Needs to Be Done)

1. Halt Deforestation and Restore Degraded Forests

- Enforce zero-deforestation laws and supply chains, especially in agriculture, mining, and infrastructure.

- Scale up reforestation and afforestation using native species.

- Expand payments for ecosystem services (PES) and carbon credits for forest preservation.

Goal: By 2027, deforestation halted and forest cover increasing in all forested countries.

2. Restore Degraded Land and Combat Desertification

- Implement land restoration programs in drylands, degraded agricultural areas, and abandoned mining zones.

- Adopt regenerative agriculture and agroforestry practices to rebuild soil health.

- Enforce Sustainable land-use planning, especially in climate-vulnerable regions.

Goal: By 2028, 50% of degraded land under active restoration.

3. Conserve Biodiversity and Protect Natural Habitats

- Expand protected areas to cover 30% of land by 2030 ("30x30" target).

- Enforce laws against illegal wildlife trade, habitat destruction, and poaching.

- Strengthen community-based and indigenous

conservation models.

Goal: By 2027, biodiversity-rich ecosystems under effective protection.

4. Integrate Ecosystem Services into Development Planning

- Include ecosystem valuation in National economic planning, budgeting, and infrastructure decisions.

- Mandate environmental impact assessments (EIAs) for all major development projects.

- Prioritize nature-positive investments across agriculture, energy, and transport.

Goal: By 2026, ecosystem services mainstreamed into National planning systems.

5. Strengthen Climate-Nature Synergies

- Implement nature-based solutions for climate mitigation and adaptation (e.g., wetlands, mangroves, forests).

- Align National climate commitments (NDCs) with biodiversity and land restoration goals.

- Protect high-carbon ecosystems (peatlands, mangroves, old-growth forests).

Goal: By 2027, nature-based climate solutions integrated in 100% of National climate plans.

B. Operational Mechanisms (How to Deliver the Strategies)

1. Strengthen Land and Biodiversity Governance

- Enact or update National Biodiversity Strategies and

Action Plans (NBSAPs).

- Harmonize land-use, forestry, agriculture, and environmental policies.

- Recognize and secure indigenous and community land rights.

Timeline: Strong National biodiversity governance systems operational by 2026.

2. Mobilize Finance for Restoration and Conservation

- Launch Land Restoration Investment Platforms and Green Bonds tied to SDG 15 outcomes.

- Redirect agricultural subsidies toward regenerative land use and conservation agriculture.

- Include nature in climate finance allocations.

Timeline: Nature-positive public and private finance scaled by 2027.

3. Build Data and Monitoring Systems for Biodiversity and Land Health

- Use satellite monitoring, AI, and geospatial data to track forest cover, soil health, and biodiversity trends.

- Establish National biodiversity observatories and reporting dashboards.

Timeline: SDG 15 monitoring systems active in all regions by 2026.

4. Support Indigenous and Community-Based Conservation

- Provide funding and legal protection for indigenous land

stewardship.

- Strengthen local conservation institutions with capacity-building and co-management rights.

Timeline: Indigenous and local conservation areas formally recognized in at least 75 countries by 2027.

5. Educate and Mobilize Public Action for Nature

- Integrate biodiversity and land restoration Education into National curricula.

- Launch National campaigns for tree planting, wildlife protection, and land care.

- Encourage citizen science and youth-led conservation projects.

Timeline: National nature Education programs launched in all countries by 2026.

In Summary: Fast-Track Priorities for SDG 15 (Life on Land)

Priority Area	Goal by 2030
Halt deforestation	Net deforestation stopped Globally
Restore degraded land	50% of degraded land restored
Protect biodiversity and habitats	30% of land under effective protection
Align with climate goals	Nature-based solutions in all National plans
Secure indigenous rights and participation	Legal recognition and funding support scaled
Finance, monitoring, and governance	All countries with SDG 15-aligned action systems

Visual Roadmap: Reaching SDG 15 (Life on Land) Targets by 2030

[Timeline Layout: Horizontal — milestones year-by-year from 2025 to 2030]

2025: Foundation Year – Governance, Finance, and Legal Reform

- Launch or update National Biodiversity Strategies and Action Plans (NBSAPs).

- Enact land-use policies and legal frameworks to halt deforestation and recognize indigenous land rights.

- Establish National green finance platforms for land restoration and ecosystem conservation.

2026: Forest and Land Restoration Acceleration

- Scale reforestation and afforestation programs using native species.

- Launch National campaigns for regenerative agriculture and agroforestry.

- Deploy satellite systems to monitor land degradation and forest cover.

2027: Biodiversity Protection and Ecosystem Services Integration

- Expand protected areas to reach 30% of National land territory.

- Strengthen enforcement of anti-poaching and wildlife trafficking laws.

- Integrate ecosystem valuation into National economic and infrastructure planning.

2028: Climate-Nature Synergies and Community Conservation

- Implement nature-based solutions for flood prevention, drought resilience, and carbon sequestration.

- Fully embed ecosystem protection into National climate plans (NDCs).

- Scale up community-led conservation and indigenous co-management programs.

2029: Global Knowledge Sharing and Final Acceleration Push

- Publish restoration and biodiversity protection best practices for Global replication.

- Accelerate cross-border cooperation on ecosystem corridors, migratory species, and transboundary conservation.

- Finalize National SDG 15 reporting frameworks.

2030: Achievement of SDG 15 Goals

- Global deforestation halted and land degradation reversed.

- 30% of land effectively protected and managed.

- Biodiversity thriving, ecosystems restored, and nature aligned with climate and development goals.

Strategies and Operational Mechanisms to Achieve SDG 16: Peace, Justice and Strong Institutions by 2030

A. Strategies (What Needs to Be Done)

1. Promote Transparent, Accountable, and Inclusive Governance

- Strengthen public institutions through digitalization, open data, and citizen feedback mechanisms.

- Promote participatory policy-making and inclusive electoral systems.

- Expand open government partnerships to improve responsiveness.

Goal: By 2026, transparency and accountability frameworks institutionalized in all public sectors.

2. Ensure Universal Access to Justice

- Expand legal aid systems for the poor, women, children, and marginalized groups.

- Establish community-based dispute resolution mechanisms and mobile courts.

- Integrate gender-sensitive justice services, especially for victims of GBV and domestic violence.

Goal: By 2027, all countries provide basic legal services and justice access at the community level.

3. Strengthen Rule of Law and Legal Systems

- Modernize and digitize court systems, case tracking, and legal databases.

- Train law enforcement, prosecutors, and judiciary in human rights, anti-discrimination, and due process.

- Combat pre-trial detention overuse and promote restorative justice models.

Goal: By 2028, fair trial standards met in all National justice systems.

4. Combat Corruption and Illicit Financial Flows

- Enforce anti-corruption laws, whistleblower protections, and asset recovery frameworks.

- Strengthen beneficial ownership transparency and public procurement integrity.

- Enhance International cooperation to combat tax evasion and organized crime.

Goal: By 2027, measurable reduction in illicit financial flows and public-sector corruption.

5. Build Peaceful, Inclusive, and Safe Societies

- Implement violence prevention strategies, especially for youth, women, and conflict-prone areas.

- Invest in police reform and community policing.

- Address root causes of conflict: inequality, exclusion, and weak institutions.

Goal: By 2026, significant reduction in homicide, gender-based violence, and civil unrest.

B. Operational Mechanisms (How to Deliver the Strategies)

1. Strengthen Institutional Capacity and Public Sector Integrity

- Deploy civil service reform strategies to build merit-based, ethical, and professional public institutions.

- Introduce integrity audits and accountability scorecards across government levels.

Timeline: Public sector integrity systems operational in all countries by 2026.

2. Scale Up Digital Tools for Governance and Justice

- Use e-governance platforms for service delivery, licensing, budgeting, and procurement.

- Introduce AI-driven legal diagnostics, online dispute resolution, and digital legal literacy tools.

Timeline: Smart justice and digital governance platforms live by 2027 in most countries.

3. Increase Investment in Justice and Rule of Law

- Prioritize justice sector funding in National budgets.

- Establish justice innovation funds for legal startups and grassroots legal empowerment.

Timeline: Justice budget share and access financing increased Globally by 2026.

4. Enhance Civic Engagement and Protect Human Rights

- Support civil society and media freedom through legal

protections and financial sustainability.

- Protect human rights defenders, journalists, and civic activists from retaliation.

Timeline: National laws aligned with civic and media rights frameworks by 2026.

5. Monitor Institutional Performance and SDG 16 Metrics

- Develop real-time governance and justice dashboards to monitor service delivery, complaints, and human rights violations.

- Use disaggregated data (gender, age, ethnicity, location) for inclusive performance tracking.

Timeline: National SDG 16 monitoring systems fully operational by 2027.

In Summary: Fast-Track Priorities for SDG 16 (Peace, Justice, Strong Institutions)

Priority Area	Goal by 2030
Transparent and accountable governance	Institutionalized in public sectors Globally
Equal access to justice	Legal services accessible to all communities
Rule of law and legal reform	Fair trial, digitized legal systems in place
Anti-corruption and IFF control	Major progress in financial integrity
Peacebuilding and violence reduction	Safer societies, reduced homicide and GBV
Civic rights and institutional trust	Civic space open and protected in all countries

Tone for 2025–2030:

Rights-Based, Institution-Focused, Integrity-Driven, Justice-Led, Peace-Enabling.

2025: Foundation Year – Governance Reform and Legal Access Expansion

- Launch transparency and anti-corruption initiatives (open data, integrity audits, digital procurement).

- Expand legal aid services and community justice systems.

- Update National justice strategies with a focus on inclusion and digital reform.

2026: Rule of Law, Public Sector Integrity, and Civic Engagement

- Train law enforcement and judiciary in human rights and non-discrimination.

- Strengthen protections for human rights defenders and journalists.

- Implement public sector accountability scorecards across ministries.

2027: Digital Justice, Dispute Resolution, and Institutional Performance Tracking

- Launch e-courts, online dispute resolution, and mobile legal services.

- Operationalize National SDG 16 monitoring dashboards with disaggregated data.

- Scale community policing and restorative justice models.

2028: Combat Illicit Financial Flows and Protect Public Resources

- Enforce whistleblower protection and asset recovery systems.

- Track and reduce illicit financial flows through transparency in ownership and financial disclosures.

- Strengthen International legal cooperation and anti-money laundering frameworks.

2029: Conflict Prevention, Peacebuilding, and Final Acceleration Push

- Implement violence prevention strategies in high-risk communities.

- Support cross-border cooperation on justice, conflict resolution, and institution building.

- Finalize National and regional progress reviews of SDG 16 indicators.

2030: Achievement of SDG 16 Goals

- Universal access to justice and strong, transparent institutions.

- Corruption significantly reduced and civic trust restored.

- Peaceful, inclusive societies protected by fair laws and accountable governance.

SDG 17: Partnerships for the Goals, the final but absolutely critical enabler for achieving all other SDGs. Without stronger partnerships — between governments, business, civil society, and International institutions — the SDG agenda cannot be delivered.

Here's the full strategies and operational mechanisms guide to achieve SDG 17 in the next five years:

Strategies and Operational Mechanisms to Achieve SDG 17: Partnerships for the Goals by 2030

A. Strategies (What Needs to Be Done)

1. Strengthen Finance Mobilization for Sustainable Development

- Scale up domestic resource mobilization (DRM) — fair taxation systems, efficient public finance.

- Expand International support — climate finance, concessional financing, blended finance instruments.

- Increase access to finance for low-income and developing countries.

Goal: By 2026, significant increase in Sustainable finance flows for SDG achievement.

2. Facilitate Access to Technology, Innovation, and Knowledge Sharing

- Support technology transfer platforms and expand access to affordable digital technologies.

- Promote South-South and Triangular cooperation on innovation and capacity-building.

- Advance open science, digital public goods, and data-sharing initiatives.

Goal: By 2027, universal access to key Sustainable development technologies and innovations.

3. Build Stronger Multistakeholder Partnerships

- Foster cross-sector partnerships: governments + business + academia + civil society working together.

- Promote public-private partnerships (PPPs) for infrastructure, health, Education, and green projects.

- Strengthen Global SDG platforms to share knowledge, align investments, and coordinate action.

Goal: By 2026, multisector SDG partnerships operational in every country.

4. Support Capacity Building in Developing and Fragile States

- Expand technical assistance, training, and institutional development for least-developed countries (LDCs), small island developing states (SIDS), and conflict-affected areas.

- Build local capacity to implement, monitor, and evaluate SDG programs.

Goal: By 2027, 100% of developing countries benefit from SDG capacity-building programs.

5. Enhance Data, Monitoring, and Accountability Systems

- Build National statistical capacities to track SDG progress effectively.

- Support open data platforms and SDG tracking dashboards for public use.

- Implement multi-stakeholder SDG accountability frameworks at National and Global levels.

Goal: By 2026, all countries publish annual, transparent SDG progress reports.

B. Operational Mechanisms (How to Deliver the Strategies)

1. Launch Global and Regional Financing Initiatives

- Expand the role of Green Climate Fund, SDG Impact Fund, and Sustainable Development Investment Platforms.

- Create National SDG financing strategies aligned with integrated National development plans.

Timeline: National SDG financing frameworks operational Globally by 2026.

2. Operationalize Technology and Knowledge Partnerships

- Establish regional SDG Innovation Hubs, linking startups, universities, policymakers, and funders.

- Accelerate the deployment of digital public infrastructure (open-source digital ID, payment systems, data sharing).

Timeline: Technology hubs and knowledge-sharing platforms live by 2027.

3. Scale Public-Private Partnerships (PPPs) and Cross-Sector Collaboration

- Launch SDG Accelerator Programs bringing together companies, NGOs, cities, and multilateral agencies.

- Strengthen shared accountability frameworks for partnerships (impact reporting, transparency standards).

Timeline: SDG multistakeholder partnership ecosystems active by 2026.

4. Build Capacity and Leadership at All Levels

- Support training programs for local government officials, entrepreneurs, youth leaders, community groups on SDG implementation.
- Build local centers of excellence for SDG innovation, data science, and program management.

Timeline: Comprehensive SDG capacity-building programs operational Globally by 2027.

5. Strengthen Global SDG Accountability Mechanisms

- Support the High-Level Political Forum (HLPF) with real-time SDG data and voluntary National reviews (VNRs).
- Launch independent, citizen-led SDG monitoring platforms for grassroots accountability.

Timeline: All countries submitting enhanced VNRs and citizen reports annually by 2027.

In Summary: Fast-Track Priorities for SDG 17 (Partnerships for the Goals)

Priority Area	Goal by 2030
Finance for development	Major increase in Sustainable finance flows
Technology access and knowledge sharing	Universal access to SDG-related innovations

Multistakeholder partnerships	Strong National and Global collaboration models
Capacity-building and training	Every developing country supported
SDG data and accountability	Transparent, real-time monitoring and reporting

Visual Roadmap: Reaching SDG 17 (Partnerships for the Goals) Targets by 2030

[Timeline Layout: Horizontal — milestones year-by-year from 2025 to 2030]

2025: Foundation Year – Financing and Partnership Ecosystem Launch

- Adopt National SDG financing strategies (tax reform, SDG bonds, blended finance).

- Establish multistakeholder platforms at National and regional levels.

- Strengthen technology access for SDG-related innovation.

2026: Capacity Building, PPP Acceleration, and SDG Data Systems

- Operationalize public-private partnerships (PPPs) in energy, health, Education, and climate.

- Scale capacity-building programs for local governments, entrepreneurs, and civil society.

- Launch SDG data platforms and real-time dashboards at National levels.

2027: Technology and Innovation Hubs, Global Collaboration Deepening

- Launch SDG Innovation Hubs and regional knowledge exchange centers.

- Expand South-South cooperation and open science partnerships.

- Enable universal access to essential SDG-related digital technologies.

2028: Civic Engagement, Monitoring, and Transparency Systems Scaling

- Operationalize citizen-led SDG monitoring platforms.

- Support transparent SDG progress reporting systems across all levels of government.

- Foster inclusive digital public infrastructure for accountability and impact tracking.

2029: Final Push for Integrated Partnerships and Governance Coherence

- Align all National development plans with SDG financing and monitoring frameworks.

- Convene final regional and Global partnership summits to consolidate and share success models.

- Expand private sector SDG commitments and disclosures.

2030: Achievement of SDG 17 Goals

- Strong, inclusive partnerships delivering results across all SDGs.

- Sustainable finance and open technology systems scaled Globally.

- Transparent, accountable, and coordinated Global SDG governance architecture.

Conclusion: A Cohesive Path Forward for the SDGs

Achieving the 17 Sustainable Development Goals demands more than fragmented initiatives—it requires a cohesive, systemic strategy that aligns policy, finance, technology, and community action. To operationalize this vision, nations must embed the SDGs into national development plans, mandate corporate accountability through ESG frameworks, and mobilize blended finance to close investment gaps. Cross-sector partnerships—bridging governments, the private sector, civil society, and multilateral institutions—must be institutionalized, not improvised. Monitoring systems powered by real-time data and citizen engagement will ensure transparency and adaptability. Ultimately, delivering the SDGs hinges on political will, collaborative leadership, and a shared commitment to inclusion, resilience, and equity across generations. The pathway is complex, but the operational mechanisms are within reach—if executed with urgency and unity.

www.ingramcontent.com/pod-product-compliance
Lightning Source LLC
Chambersburg PA
CBHW071419210326
41597CB00020B/3572